STUDIES IN HISTORY, ECONOMICS AND PUBLIC LAW

EDITED BY THE FACULTY OF POLITICAL SCIENCE
OF COLUMBIA UNIVERSITY

Number 334

PROPONENTS OF LIMITED MONARCHY IN SIXTEENTH CENTURY FRANCE:

FRANCIS HOTMAN AND JEAN BODIN

PROPONENTS OF LIMITED MONARCHY IN SIXTEENTH CENTURY FRANCE: FRANCIS HOTMAN AND JEAN BODIN

BY

BEATRICE REYNOLDS

AMS PRESS
NEW YORK

COLUMBIA UNIVERSITY
STUDIES IN THE
SOCIAL SCIENCES

334

The Series was formerly known as
Studies in History, Economics and Public Law.

Reprinted with the permission of Columbia University Press
From the edition of 1931, New York
First AMS EDITION published 1968
Manufactured in the United States of America

Library of Congress Catalogue Card Number: 68-58616

AMS PRESS, INC.
NEW YORK, N.Y. 10003

TABLE OF CONTENTS

INTRODUCTION

Part I

The increasing absolutism of their monarch did not pass unquestioned by French publicists in the later middle age. Face to face with a power which was restrained only by the mild hand of precedent, courageous spirits like Philip Pot yet dared to affirm that the prince existed only by the will of the people; [1] or to ask like Commines, "Is there a lord upon earth who dares to take a penny from his subjects without their consent, unless by tyranny?" Or earlier still, to address the king himself with these words: "C'est grant chose que d'estre roy ou prince; mais est encores plus grant chose de soubzmettre à raison et aux loys le royaume." [2]

In earlier Capetian days, when the realm of France included only the upper valleys of the Seine and the Loire, when the king lived upon the proceeds of his domain, and was merely first among many feudal lords, he was the owner of the land, and, as such, the dispenser of justice to all the dwellers thereon. He was their natural protector, the leader of the feudal host, and from him all authority flowed down. To the praepositi (prévôts) he delegated a share of this indeterminate power, but mindful of the usurpations of the great nobles who, in Carolingian times, had contrived to make their benefices hereditary, he selected officials of humbler origin for his domain.

[1] Jehan Masselin, *Journal des États Généraux de Tours,* Edition Bernier (Paris, 1835), vol. i, p. 146.

[2] Jean Juvénal des Ursins, *Epître au roi Charles VII*, Ms. Fr. 2701 Fol. 97 r° quoted in Paul Viollet, *Histoire des institutions politiques et administratives de la France* (Paris, 1890), vol. iii, p. 227.

To assist him in the many occupations of a great landowner, he had, as every major baron had, an advisory council, made up of tenants-in-chief, both lay and clerical, to whom might be added anyone else particularly helpful,—it was not the day of the specialist. This curia was deliberative, auxiliary to the king, ever open for consultation, without legal right to oppose. But it would have been a rash monarch indeed who would follow a course in the teeth of the disapproval of his important vassals. The seneschal, later, the chancellor, headed the group; from the collective body were to spring many offshoots, as multiplicity of function, under increasing burdens, gave way to differentiation.

Denial or abuse of justice permitted an appeal from the court of the baron to that of the king. Evocations and the special privileges of the bourgeoisie du roi contrived to swell the total number of cases. In the latter part of the reign of Philip Augustus, the curia regis resolved itself into three subsidiary branches, administrative, judicial and financial. There was no sharp distinction as to personnel or sphere, but the supervision of royal revenue was usually exercised by the Chambre des Comptes, at the Temple; the Palais Royal of the Cité sheltered both the Parlement and the administrative body, which now occasionally took the title Grand Conseil. In theory, the king presided over each of these; the patriarchal semi-divine conception of the monarch as giver of justice still persevered. Actually the standardisation of forms, an increasing knowledge of customary law and of accounting, and the multifarious concerns of an ever-growing territory made his personal direction impossible. Parlement itself could not deal with all the business referred to it. Before 1278, there were three different Chambers, and in the next century, a fourth, the Cour des Aides.

In the domain, a similar specialisation was taking place. The despotism of the prévôt had necessitated the superimposition of another official, the bailli, at the time of the Third Crusade. He was theoretically a member of the curia, bearing to the bailliage the commands of the king, and in this capacity resembling the *missi dominici* of the Carolingian period. In addition to financial and military functions, he had important judicial powers, which enabled him to hold periodical assizes in the chief town of the district. The existence of these officials, like that of the circuit judges in England, had a tendency toward unification of the law, since they represented the central government and made every effort to attract cases from the lower courts to their own. As the bailli was noble, but the prévôt roturier, it followed that any case involving a person of rank must be tried in the court of the bailli. But when law became more intricate, requiring special knowledge, the exercise of the judicial functions was delegated by the bailli to a lieutenant who ultimately succeeded to this prerogative by royal decree. Later the military powers of the bailli were bestowed elsewhere; in the lapse of two hundred years, five subsidiaries had succeeded to the various activities of this surveying functionary, and the bailli, in the words of Viollet, was taking the path towards decorative inutility.

The development of the curia regis in France bears so striking a similarity to the situation in thirteenth-century England that one can hardly fail to ask "Which influenced the other?" or "Were conditions in western Europe so much alike that growth naturally took place along the same lines, without any dependence or contact?" There was at least one definite tie between the two countries, for at the beginning of the thirteenth century, certain fiefs reverted to the crown, of which Normandy was the most important. How far did Norman institutions affect France? How far did they affect England? Neither question has been answered definitely, but it is difficult not to assume that the duchy on the

Channel was a connecting link between the administrative forms of the two kingdoms, particularly when we consider such special institutions as the English Exchequer, the Norman Exchequer, and the Chambre des Comptes, with the supplementary, judicial Cour des Aides. It was a fortunate coincidence that Normandy should become French at a time (1202) when the reigning king was a man of vigor and initiative.

The curia regis, relieved of most of its judicial and financial labors, continued to assist the king in the exercise of his second great prerogative, the making of law. This must have been declaratory of custom until the reign of Philip III, when Languedoc, with its written law, became part of France. The gradual infiltration of the Roman doctrine increased the tendency toward introductory law, but the king "could not violate anything done in the past, nor anything to come, in the period for which the law was good".[1] Beaumanoir adds that the monarch should take care, in the preparation of new institutions, that his innovations have a reasonable cause, that they be to the profit of all, and duly approved by the Grand Council; and especially that "they should not be in violation of God, nor contrary to good usage, for . . . . his subjects ought not to suffer since each one, above all things, ought to love and fear God with all his heart".[2]

The flexibility of the curia led to important constitutional developments. As the scope of an ordinance increased, in range of territory affected, and in penetration of central authority, so did the membership of the advisory body increase. The officers of the king's household formed the council when the administration of the domain was under discussion; for minor matters concerning the realm, representative barons

[1] Beaumanoir, *Coustumes de Beauvaisis*, Edition Beugnot (Paris, 1842), vol. ii, p. 262.

[2] *Ibid.*, p. 263.

from various sections were invited to attend; but when the situation became critical, an appeal to confer with their sovereign was made to all parts of the kingdom. The quarrel with Boniface VIII, which involved not only the matter of taxation, but indirectly the question of a national church and divine origin of kingship, led Philip IV to seek support from every class in his kingdom. Feudal customs had set a precedent for the summoning of noble vassals, both lay and clerical, to render *auxilium et consilium*. To add burghers to the group was unusual, but as the king was not certain of the loyalty of the clergy, it was necessary to counterbalance their vote. On the tenth of April, 1302, deputies from the three orders met in the cathedral of Notre Dame, and decided to approve the king's policy. The tactics by which he obtained this approval were to be sure little calculated to train the deputies in the responsibilities of administration,[1] but the introduction of the burghers into the central government is sufficient indication that the king was aware of the advancing power of the bonnes villes. He convoked the three estates in 1308, to consider the charges against the Knights Templars which led to the suppression of that Order, and again in 1314, for subsidies to carry on the war in Flanders. At this time only members of the bourgeoisie and of religious chapters were elected to serve as deputies; nobles and princes of the Church received a summons because of their rank.

Legislative power was divided between the king and his council, with the greater emphasis upon the royal share.[2]

[1] *Cf.* G. Picot, *Histoire des États Généraux* (Paris, 1872), vol. i, p. 22. It is interesting to observe that an assembly was summoned to Pamiers in 1212 by Simon de Montfort, to which prominent burghers were invited. The meeting of the three estates in 1302, while the most important of those convoked by Philip IV, was not the first. See Henri Martin, *Histoire de France* (Paris, 1858), vol. v, p. 23, footnote.

[2] N. Valois, "Le Gouvernement représentatif en France au XIVe siècle," *Revue des Questions Historiques*, XXXVI (1885) 64.

Yet apparently the king could not make law without the presence of the councillors, and their consent was implicit. The composition of the group in each case determined the extent to which their traditional right was exercised. If they were stout-hearted men, they might dare to deny their lord; if they were weak, it was just possible for any monarch to be absolute, within the limits of the only constitutional check; in consideration of his somewhat straightened means, even Philip the Fair found absolutism impossible. The removal of this material obstacle of financial stress was in part the cause of the summons to the wealthy burghers; in the effort to make himself supreme, the king found it necessary to share with still another group some of the attributes of sovereignty.

The fourteenth century saw a rapid, indeed precocious, development of the Estates General, which was very closely parallel to the establishment in England of that attempted constitutional government which died with Richard II and the Lancastrian revolt. Under the weak sons of Philip the Fair, an effort was made to diminish the royal predominance by opposing to it a check formed by the aristocracy.[1] The most unpopular minister of the former king was removed from office, at the request of all the barons, and a council composed of members selected by the nobles was forced upon Louis X. It was at this period also that Normandy obtained its Grande Charte (1315) granting immunity from taxation except by the consent of its own provincial Estates.

These changes, interesting though they may be, had but a short life, due to the outbreak of war with England. Eighteen years of intermittent compaigning were generally unfavorable to France. She had suffered the disasters of Crécy and Calais, her nobility had been decimated, the gov-

[1] *Cf.* England under Edward II.

ernment was bankrupt. In order to obtain funds the central administration debased the currency; then the king declared a moratorium on royal accounts; finally, in December, 1355, he called the Estates General. Discontent with the administration of the war had driven the deputies to adopt a firmer attitude, and to bargain for redress of grievances before granting supplies. They voted five millions of pounds for the maintenance of thirty thousand men at arms, on condition (1) that the collection and disbursement of the funds should be in the hands of agents appointed by the Estates; (2) that all classes, even the royal family, should be liable to the tax; (3) that the deputies should reassemble, without further convocation, twice within the ensuing year; (4) that no decision of any two orders should be binding upon an unwilling third.

Under happier circumstances, this would have delivered the financial administration into the hands of the three estates, but the course of the war made orderly government impossible. Some of the wealthiest provinces were so harassed by the enemy that tax returns were insufficient and, driven to desperate straits, John (the Good!) again had recourse to debasement of the currency. The crowning calamity of Poitiers (1356) was the occasion for an outburst of popular indignation. The king was a prisoner, his heir (the Duke of Normandy), a youth of but twenty years, the treasury empty, the English marching into the heart of France. In such a crisis, the young duke was advised to appeal to the nation for aid and counsel. His father's ineptitude, and the selfseeking policy of the councillors by whom he was surrounded, had brought the kingdom to so low an ebb, that unconsciously the concept of the kingship was altered. Was there anything patriarchal or divine about a monarch whose plans had led to impoverishment and defeat? Was he the protector of his people, the wise maker of laws? Men of the chartered towns, who had by prudent management brought their communities from insignificant trading centers to the dignity of representation in the Estates, were not content to leave all authority in hands obviously incapable, and they came to Paris with a well defined desire of reform (October, 1356).

The assembly was unusually large, more than eight hundred members meeting in the Palais de Justice. Of these about half were of the third estate, since the ranks of the nobility had been thinned in battle. The absence of the barons, who had taken the initiative in 1315, must explain the more democratic tinge in the tenor of the policies advocated by the Estates in 1356. Their first object of attack was the council. The regent had suggested that some of its members might be present with the deputies in their deliberations, but this assistance was politely declined. After conferences lasting a fortnight, the Committee of Eighty requested a private interview with the Dauphin. He was thereupon informed that the miseries of the kingdom were charged upon those who had ill-advised the king, and that the deputies asked the dismissal, arrest and confiscation of property of many of these councillors. They did not hesitate to name the first President of Parlement, and the Archbishop of Rouen, Chancellor of France. The council was accused, not so much of bad judgment, as of lack of patriotism, — "de n'avoir eu égard . . . ni à la crainte de Dieu, ni à l'honneur du souverain, ni à la misère des peuples; de n'avoir eu en vue que leur interêt particulier. . . ." [1] In view of the fact that the council could do nothing without the consent, probably without the initiative, of the king, it is surprising that the Estates should have protected him by the interposition of a doctrine strangely like that of ministerial responsibility. Although he was supreme, still the blame was placed upon the counsellors. They were to be handed over for trial to commissioners elected by

[1] Fragment from Villaret quoted in Picot, *op. cit.*, vol. i, p. 48.

the Estates, and in their stead were to be chosen twenty-eight deputies from all three orders, without whose advice the Duke of Normandy could take no step. If we combine with this the reiterated demand for frequent spontaneous meetings of the Estates, we have something very like cabinet government. Confronted with so radical a diminution of authority, the Dauphin took fright, and dismissed the Estates without obtaining a subsidy. They departed reluctantly, after a final meeting in which they agreed to report to their constituents the reforms they had advocated and the action of the regent.

Public opinion in Paris favored the deputies, and as the provinces learned of the course of events, their sympathy also was won over to the popular viewpoint. Although practically all the country was in a state of irritation against him, the Dauphin had the temerity to pass a new issue of depreciated currency which should provide funds for the government. When the indignant populace found that they were once more accepting a forced loan, riots broke out. At the head of a mob, Etienne Marcel compelled the lieutenant of the regent to postpone the issue of new coins. Continual tumults and disorder in the capital forced the Dauphin to the realisation that resistance was useless; he summoned the Estates to reconvene, and for the third time in fifteen months, the accusing face of the nation looked upon its natural protector, and found him lacking. Then they took upon themselves the initiative and the burden of reform. Their first act was a referendum to all the northern provinces of the remonstrances from the former Committee of Eighty. With truly remarkable expedition, these were delivered, discussed, and, in less than a month, returned to Paris with the full approval of the local bodies. Strengthened by this definite mandate, the Estates renewed the demands of the previous October, and the Dauphin, seeing no other course available, signed an ordinance embodying the cahiers of the last three sessions. It is uncertain whether the royal council composed of the nominees of the Estates ever actually existed,[1] but the patriotic labors of the deputies failed in this instance, as on former occasions. Expensive and repeated journeys to and from the capitol cooled the ardor of many. Each succeeding assembly grew smaller. There was in addition the turbulence of the revolutionary element in Paris which intimidated many conservative reformers, and darkened the progressive movement by the charge of treason to the House of Valois. The followers of Marcel, intoxicated by their power, despotic in its use, abandoned the principle of constitutional liberty which had guided the patriots at the outset of the struggle. They used their authority more autocratically than the king had used his, and not more wisely. With the assassination of Marcel, the last barricade was gone, and the king returned to his own.

Although his sovereignty was unquestioned throughout a reign of sixteen years, Charles V was not a tyrant. He had profited by the experiences of his youth, and endeavored to rule his people wisely, possibly in order to save himself greater trouble. At his death France was left in a situation very similar to that in which she found herself after Poitiers; royalty was represented by a minor,—in this case a boy of twelve,—there were disputes as to the regency, and resistance to the collection of taxes. A long period of civil war followed by an English invasion produced so calamitous a state that another attempt was made to transfer the reins of government from the hands of the quarrelsome princes to a more democratic control. The crisis of 1413 was distinguished from the others by the leading role played by repre-

[1] Affirmative view in Picot, *Histoire des États Généraux; Grande Encyclopédie*, Article " État " (C. V. Langlois). Negative view in Valois, " Le Gouvernement représentatif . . . ", *Revue des Questions Historiques*, XXXVI (1885) 63.

sentatives of the University of Paris, one of whom drew up a complete statement of the evils of the reign and of the remedies which should be applied thereto. The resulting ordinance arranged for reorganisation of the judicial and financial systems of the nation, but made no provision for retaining control of the executive. It had as short a life as that issued in 1357.

The next seventy years cover a period in which hardly a flicker of political liberty illumined the darkness of defeat, renewed warfare, and crafty despotism. Constant drain of men and money reduced the vitality and enthusiasm of the nation to so low a pitch that the Estates no longer attempted to bargain for reforms. They had learned to pay, and to submit. They even granted to Charles VII a permanent tax (1436) appropriated to the army, without introducing safeguards to ensure its proper application. From that time, the monarchy, by the exercise of even the mildest economy, could have made itself independent of the Estates. That it did not achieve this was due more to the prodigal bestowal of pensions, the spendthrift magnificence of the court, and a childish fondness for offensive warfare, than to an obdurate spirit of liberty on the part of the bourgeoisie. The Estates of Tours, in preparation for the repulse of a rebellion led by the Duke of Brittany, granted to Louis XI " que le roi, sans attendre aucune assemblée, ne congregation des États, qui ne se peuvent pas aisément assembler, y puisse faire tout ce que ordre de justice le porte, promettant iceux États. . . . d'obéir " [1] This was exactly in accordance with the wishes of Louis, as revealed by Commines; [2] within a short space of

[1] Picot, *op. cit.*, vol. i, p. 350. [From the procès verbal in Isambert, *Les Ordonnances des rois de France* (Paris, 1822), vol. viii, p. 731, where it is falsely attributed to an earlier date.]

[2] Philippe de Commines, *Mémoires*, Edition Maudrot (Paris, 1901), vol. i, p. 178.

time he twice summoned the Estates, which he had never done before, and never did again, but he invited to the assembly only specified men, and those who he thought would not contradict his wishes. It was a feigned appeal to the nation made to outwit the leaders of the League of Public Weal. Despite his high-handed ways, Louis was of real service to France, in obtaining for her by chicane or otherwise several outlying fiefs [1] and in crushing the last remnants of a quarrelsome nobility. The old theory of divine appointment, hiding somewhere in the background, was refurbished and brought forward to defend his personal rule. Quizzical, superstitious, and solitary, Louis trusted no one, not even his children, and guided his kingdom through peril with the watchword *nosce dissimulare.*

There was a sigh of relief at his death. The lower classes hoped for abatement of taxation; the nobility, to win back what it had lost of power. While the new king was merely a boy, nevertheless his governors, the daughter and son-in-law of Louis, were sufficiently versed in their father's tactics to manipulate the situation to the advantage of the monarchy. They did, it is true, summon the Estates to Tours immediately upon the accession of Charles VIII, but by shifting the electoral arrangements [2] they contrived so to weaken class solidarity that relatively little was accomplished in the assembly. An attempt was made again to complete the council by the addition of a dozen members from the Estates. The number dwindled eventually to three,—too small a group to produce any democratic tinge in the advisory body which remained the meeting ground of former satellites of Louis and of the recent adherents of his daughter. A more effective effort resulted in the reform of the judiciary, which thenceforward, by a process of co-option, presented to the king three nominees for each vacancy.

[1] Burgundy, Provence, Maine, Anjou, Bar.

[2] Viollet, *op. cit.*, vol. iii, p. 229.

The finances of the kingdom were subjected to severe criticism; a request was made for an exact statement of the receipts from the royal domain, and of the aides, because it was difficult to judge of the size of grant needed, until the assembly was informed concerning the usual income. At this time the advantageous position of Normandy, Burgundy, and Languedoc was the object of comment. In giving subsidies, none of these provinces was affected by the decision of the assembly as a whole. Each preserved, at least in theory, the right to submit such impositions for the approval of its own provincial Estates. The great charter of 1315 had confirmed such a privilege to the Normans, and Charles VIII, in a letter to their Estates, had recently recognized similar rights of the Burgundians " de toute ancienneté, et par privilège confirmés et jurés par iceux prédécesseurs".[1] At Tours, the suggestion was made, though it went no further, that it would be well to remodel the entire kingdom on this plan. The deputies were pathetically in earnest in the execution of their task. Their duty was to give counsel and advice to the king; they interpreted this to include the right of criticism, and made an exhaustive report upon maladministration and inefficiency, with wise recommendations for correction. It was not an intelligent appreciation of good and bad government which they lacked, it was rather the ability, " political " in a more modern sense, to gather together a majority capable of sinking its minor differences, and imposing its wishes upon the whole. According to Masselin, who was of course not impartial, the deputies of Normandy and Burgundy were able to unite but were thwarted by the action of the Parisian delegates.

It is interesting to learn that at this meeting occurred a

[1] *Recueil de pièces originales et authentiques concernant la tenue des États Généraux* (Paris, 1789), vol. iii, p. 340. For Languedoc see Picot, *op. cit.*, vol. i, p. 538.

theoretical discussion as to the constitutional position of the Estates,[1] in which some deputies maintained that the sovereignty (*totam regni summam*) had fallen to the Estates: that it was not needful for them to make supplication, but rather that they should command at least until they should have established a council which might receive its sovereignty (*summam potestatem*) from them. Others felt that, during the minority, the right to command was a prerogative of the princes of the blood, and that the approval of the Estates had to be sought only in the levy of tribute. The outcome of their discussion was the long speech of Philip Pot, a noble deputy from Burgundy, of which the general tenor is indicated in the first paragraph of this introduction.

The reign of Louis XII (1498-1515) was marked by no constitutional development. Cessation of civil war, resulting in a period of commercial prosperity fostered by prudent legislation, won the approval of the bourgeoisie and the poorer classes. A stabilised currency, removal of many vexatious duties formerly levied along the river courses, an increasing amount of land brought under cultivation, and the creation of local parlements in Normandy, Provence and Burgundy eliminated the chief causes of dissatisfaction. There were certain administrative reforms with regard to Parlementary procedure and the functioning of the financial bodies, which made no fundamental alteration in the government, but testified to the careful supervision exercised by Louis and his minister, Georges d'Amboise. The king regarded himself as "débiteur de justice à nos subiets"[2] and in this capacity won their grateful affection. Seventy years later, Bodin could say of him, "Oh excellent prince, worthy of the rule of the whole world! Who, relying upon the integrity and harmlessness of his life, feared not the maledictions of the

[1] Masselin, *op. cit.*, vol. i, p. 138.

[2] Isambert, *op. cit.*, vol. xi, p. 296.

wicked!"[1] It was a brief return to the patriarchal monarchy.

Seyssel, writing in 1519, thought that he discovered three checks upon the royal power,—those of religion, justice, and polity. Following the same order, he explains that it is permitted to any clerical to remonstrate with the king upon his conduct, even to reproach him publicly. Royal rescripts must obtain the final approval of Parlement, which has been instituted chiefly for the purpose of restraining absolutism, and whose members are in an excellent position to fulfill this function, since their term of office is for life. Finally, the king is checked by the ordinances of his predecessors. If he should violate these hallowed traditions, no one would obey his commands. Seyssel adds that the largess of the princes is restrained by the careful supervision of the chambre des comptes.

It is difficult to credit this account of the monarchy under Louis XII. It is far more likely that the author was making a plea to the new king, Francis I, for less munificence, and greater consideration of the traditions behind the institutions. His wish seems to have been for a monarchy tempered by the approval of Parlement, which he pictures thus:

Laquelle [la monarchie] n'en est pour ce, moindre, mais d'autant est plus digne, qu'elle est mieux reglée. Et si elle estait plus ample et absolue, elle en serait pire et plus imparfaicte. . . . Et sont les roys beaucoup plus à louer, et priser de ce qu'ils veullent en si grande auctorité et puissance estre subiectz à leurs propres loix et vivre selon icelles, que s'ils pouvaient à leur volonté user de puissance absolue.[2]

In concluding this rapid survey of the early constitutional

[1] Jean Bodin, *Methodus ad facilem historiarum cognitionem* (Lyons, 1583), p. 263.

[2] Seyssel, *La grant monarchie de France* (Paris, 1541), p. 16 r°.

history of France, we are faced with three outstanding facts: (1) that there was, at any rate in the fourteenth century, a vigorous spirit of political liberty, which contested hotly the abuse of sovereignty, (2) that the course of the struggle, in the attitude of the separate classes, in the demands made, and in the actual legislation passed, bore a striking resemblance to contemporaneous developments in England, (3) that in the case of France there were certain psychological, geographical and historical factors, non-existent in the case of the other nation, which materially impeded her constitutional progress.

An effective check could have been placed upon the growth of absolutism if the granting of taxes by the Estates had been a necessary preliminary to the collection of money by royal officials. It would have been a further advantage if they had been able to maintain a continuous system of election to office, and a recognised right to investigate and punish administrative abuses. Finally, if they could have retained control of the executive and legislative branches by the appointment of a council, they would have deprived the king of all initiative in resistance, of all chance of extravagance or favoritism, and of any opportunity to follow, for a prolonged period, a policy contrary to popular wishes. *All of these expedients were attempted in the period 1315-1484.*

Just as the first resistance in England developed among the barons so in France, exactly a century later, they were the first to throw themselves into opposition. They went further than the lords of 1215, who won a promise of good government and authorisation to rebel against tyranny. The French barons tried to make their nominees part of the government. As commercial prosperity increased the wealth of the burghers in both countries, so did the focus of resistance pass from the second to the third estate and thereby was developed a claim for sanction of fiscal levies. Becoming bolder, the deputies dared to criticise and remove the king's appointees, and to prepare a council of ministers of their own choice. In neither case was complete permanent success attained, but in neither was hope entirely abandoned.

Differences of character and temperament may have affected the ultimate establishment of a stable government. There was less of bulldog tenacity, less of stubbornness to carry their point, possibly less of sacrifice to a common advantage, in the French. Any opportunity for sympathy between the nobility and the third estate was eliminated by a class system which kept the nobleman forever apart from the bourgeois, barred off from trade or financial occupation, dedicated to martial pursuits and the maintenance of ancestral estates. Variations in opinion were multitudinous, and the abandonment of petty differences to gain a common objective was too great a tax upon the intense individualism of the deputies. The ability to scrap the unessential for the essential, to abandon the superficial for the intrinsic, might have gone a long way toward consolidating the success of rather tepid allies.

The situation was undoubtedly aggravated by the constant alterations in the geographical limits of France. Each successive assembly contained deputies from lands but recently added to the kingdom, with their own customs and traditions, at variance with other systems, and extraordinarily tenacious and jealous of interference. This particularism, while it did not prevent loyalty to the government, impeded that complete fusion of interests which alone could have won political liberty from their sometime feudal lord. Every new province was included within the political frontiers of France at the price of special concessions, so that the newest comers were in general the most advantageously placed. Then, too, the political were not the only boundaries which had to be considered. The diocese need not coincide with the French frontier, yet bishops and archbishops took their place in the gathering of the first estate. Economic ties with the Low Countries were very close, although Artois was sometimes a dependency of France, sometimes of the Empire. Compare this heterogeneity, this shifting membership, with the compactness of the English Commons after 1295.

There was also greater loyalty to the king in France. In England, the mass of the people spoke a language different from that of the court until the fourteenth century. They were of a different race, feeling an instinctive concerted hostility to a foreign ruler, whose yoke they could not throw off. Edward II they deposed; the order of succession was altered four times in a scant hundred years (1399-1485), a fact which did not pass unnoticed by French writers whose devotion to the house of Capet was tinged with something like awe. For three hundred and forty-one years the sceptre had descended in a direct line; divinely ordained, the eldest son of the Church had ruled his people. Little wonder that they hesitated to discipline him.

Introduction Part II

At the opening of the fourteenth century, the extravagant assertions of Boniface VIII led to a rupture with the French king and strengthened the claim to independence of the Gallican Church hinted at by Hincmar five hundred years before. In the lapse of another century mutual relations were determined by the Pragmatic Sanction of Bourges (1438) which deprived the Pope of the right of provisions, in returning to the chapters the privilege of election. This agreement, since it of course implied the choice of Frenchmen for bishops, made the church more national, more patriotic, and eager to maintain its representative character. At the same time, the king in weakening papal supervision, cleared the way for the monarchy by divine right, and made himself supreme within the limits of equity. He had rested beneath the spiritual guidance of the universal church, while hearkening to the temporal guidance of his curia. Now the upper restraint was largely removed, the lower, in one of its many manifestations, considerably strengthened. There were thus opposed two contradictory forces; the germ of absolutism and the germ of representative government.

Gallicanism was naturally supported by the lower clergy. Another body not directly interested in the religious question, which nevertheless favored a national church, was the Parlement. Their claim to supremacy as a court of last appeal made them antagonistic to any interference from the Papal Curia. Their position would have been affected not only in a judicial, but also in a legislative, sense since their shadowy right to correct the edicts of the king could not have been extended further. The overlordship of the Pope would have meant the diminution of their importance. Ultimately, Gallicanism found its staunchest support in Parlement, while the Sorbonne defended the rights of Rome.

The Pragmatic Sanction, in yielding power to local autonomy, impeded a policy of centralisation. Louis XI, whose goal was the elimination of any petty sovereignty, was quick to see the loophole afforded him, and by terrorising the chapters, forced them to elect his own nominees, thus completely abrogating the democratic spirit of the agreement. Despite the remonstrance of Parlement and the appeal of the Estates of Tours (1484), there were no free elections for many years. In administrative functions the king had taken the place of the Pope, who, while he could still collect revenues, recognised by the Concordat of 1516 that the right of nomination of French bishops belonged to the king of France.

But a new factor was making its appearance. The sixteenth century, which marked the flowering of humanism, saw also an awakened sense of eccleciastical abuses that penetrated into clerical and legislative circles and affected even members of the royal family. The reformers of Meaux, gathered about their bishop, Briçonnet, and Marguerite of Alençon, agitated a change in the educational system, as well as the question of clerical discipline, with a zeal for philosophic inquiry in which Francis I was very ready to join. His interest in these matters, while sincere, was nevertheless secondary to his conceptions of kingship and its prerogatives. Any change should be accomplished not from below, by the members, but from above, by the head, of the state. He made reform contingent also upon his external policy, favoring it where he wished to impede the Hapsburgs, blocking it when there was need to conciliate the Pope. As heresies from the north and east began to spread into France, Parlement and the Sorbonne joined forces to check the advance. Their persecuting tendencies, which developed before Calvinism was known, were to some extent restrained by the king, although he hardly dared to be consistent in that course.

A distrust of those portions of Roman doctrine which had been imposed by the Church fathers made itself apparent. " It is in the Holy Scriptures that Christ's doctrine is found. Do not follow the dogmas of men, which have no divine origin ", wrote Lefèvre d'Étaples, as early as 1512. He had spent his youth in philosophic inquiry which delighted him; it was not until he had passed into middle age that he became interested in the Scripture. " For a long time I was drawn to mortal studies, and had barely tasted . . . . divine . . . . but in the far distance a light shone so brightly to my sight that in comparison mortal matters seemed to me like shadows; there exhaled a perfume whose sweetness was more than earthly." [1] His life was passed in translating and commenting upon the Bible, not without great risk. The Sorbonne could not fail to be roused by passages like: " Who

[1] C. H. Graf, *La vie et les écrits de Jacques Lefèvre d'Étaples* (Strassburg, 1842) quoting the preface of Lefèvre's edition of the Psalter.

dares . . . . to say 'I will give, or I have given, satisfaction for my sins by pious works' . . . .? Oh, how thankless we are, if we do not believe that we are saved by Jesus Christ alone! . . . . Unhappy man, your salvation is not your works but the works of Christ."[1] The king's favor sheltered him until 1525. Even after that, Francis wrote from Madrid, ordering Parlement to postpone the trial,—which they declined to do. Lefèvre escaped to Germany, and returned to France only when he was assured of the protection of the king's sister. To him, in his retirement in the South, came for advice[2] one who was destined to build a mighty edifice upon his bare foundation.

It was for Calvin to organise the scattered remnants of Protestantism into a cohesive institution, to give to the anarchy prevailing among the non-Romanists a church and its government. For this his practical and legal mind was peculiarly fitted. His aim at Geneva was neither Erastian nor theocratic, but the creation of a state and a church in which the distinction between temporal and spiritual should be clearly drawn,[3] while at the same time each should lend the other support in the execution, but not the legislating, of its proper tasks. Temporal concerns were administered by the council of state; spiritual matters, by the Pastors, while the fusing of both domains created the Consistory, made up of Pastors and lay presbyters. These assemblies were partly elective. It was as though Calvin had grafted upon the medieval concept of a world ruled by Pope and Emperor, the democratic government of early Christianity. He consciously desired to return to the primitive Church, with its

[1] Graf, *op. cit.*, p. 99, quoting the *Commentary on St. John*, and the *Commentary on St. Matthew.*

[2] F. P. G. Guizot, *Les Vies de quatre grands chrétiens français* (Paris, 1873), p. 170.

[3] Guizot, *op. cit.*, pp. 267-268.

simple ritual, performed in a language known to all; an abnegation of the luxury and vices of the world, the realisation that purification was not purchasable. He succeeded in so far as he permitted the faithful to take their share of responsibility, either in the conduct of the service and singing of hymns, or in the wider activities of ecclesiastical administration; he erred where he sought to impose his own standards of morality upon the liberty of the individual mind, especially in an age characterised by a recrudescence of mental activity.

As the wave of thought passed from humanism in its various stages to Calvinism, so did it alienate itself from royal support. Francis was too self-indulgent to give over any of his favorite sins, too superstitious to renounce the opportunity of penance. In the matters of morality and justification by faith he was unsympathetic, but when the Reformed Church seemed to make an attack upon his position as absolute king, when the representative institutions of the Huguenots hinted that there were other spheres which might be affected, then indeed he abandoned them to the hostility of Parlement. The same features which antagonised the king endeared the new faith to the common people. Their poverty could not cope with the munificent charities of the nobles or bourgeoisie. If good works were essential, their chances of salvation were relatively meager. But in faith they were strong. To whom would the sufferings of a Man of the people make appeal, if not to them? As their indigence limited their generosity, so also did it confine their vices. The flock which saw a wealthy bishop expending his leisure in pastimes imitative of a corrupt court spent all its days in the harsh struggle for existence. Necessities were their luxuries; for the people of the countryside, ignorance was an extenuation of their sins. When they, dwellers in an aristocratic land, heard rumors of a church in which the service was celebrated simply in their mother tongue, whose members were worthy, where the faith of the humblest was as effective as great wealth, and in whose government such as they might share,—what wonder that the followers of Calvin were drawn largely from the rank and file of the nation.[1]

Before the death of Francis, several edicts had been passed authorising the pursuit and punishment of heretics. The preamble of one (1542) confesses that this policy has not diminished the number of dissenters. At the opening of the reign of Henry II, the new king, far more rigidly orthodox than his father, and firmly convinced that the Reform was a menace to his own power, signified his continuation of a repressive policy by the creation of a new court of Parlement, commonly called La Chambre Ardente. No one might lecture in school or university, unless he was orthodox. The possessions of all religious exiles were confiscated. Papal influence was nearly successful in procuring the introduction of the Inquisition. In retaliation and self-defense, the Protestants began to organize on the model of the Church of Geneva. Calvin was the inspiration everywhere; he sent pastors, he wrote inspiring letters, he maintained a personal interest in the fortunes of each community. A synod of at least a dozen churches met in Paris in 1559, to draw up a Confession and to agree upon ecclesiastical discipline. Despite the constant emigration, usually of scholars and industrialists whom France could not afford to lose, there was still a group large enough to create anxiety, if ever they should decide to defend their cause by arms. At the beginning of 1560 there were about 2,000,000 Huguenots in France, out of a total population of 16,000,000. The fuse was set.

[1] H. Hauser, "The French Reformation in the Sixteenth Century," *American Historical Review*, IV (1899) 217.

CHAPTER I

THE FUSION OF RELIGIOUS AND SOCIAL DISCONTENT

THE bestowal of control upon the Guises crystallised the amorphous religious and social discontent of the lower classes into a revolt with a well defined political platform, led by aristocrats.[1] Francis II was only sixteen years old at the death of his father. While he was legally of age at fourteen, he was still too weak in health and character to take full control of the government. His mother remained away from court in mourning.[2] His wife, Mary Stuart, and her uncles, the Duke of Guise and the Cardinal of Lorraine, directed the state. Montmorency, a favorite of the former king, sulked. The House of Bourbon, which stood next in line to the throne, felt defrauded of its just rights of guardianship, and in the person of Condé, a younger son, determined to vindicate them. The lower classes, suffering from a rise in prices brought about the influx of gold from the New World, turned gladly against a rule which they fancied the sole cause of their hardships. The religious fanatics, maddened by persecution, their ardor unabated, hoped that in replacing the Catholic House of Guise by the House of Bourbon, they might win not only toleration, but even a regent of their own faith. Condé had already announced his conversion, and the eldest brother, the King of Navarre, was hesitating between the two churches. By combining these vari-

[1] S. Armstrong, "Political Theory of the Huguenots," *English Historical Review* IV (1889) 13.

[2] L. Romier, *Le Royaume de Catherine de Médicis* (Paris, 1922), vol. i, p. 2.

ous groups, and using the banner of his faith as a shield for his political ambitions, Condé contrived to create a party [1] which, after the vicissitudes and civil wars of a quarter century, ultimately won its way to the throne, not without the sacrifice of some principles loudly proclaimed on the march.

A rumor was circulated that the king was held a prisoner in his castle of Amboise by the Duke of Guise, and loyal Frenchmen were urged to his rescue. Reinforcements in men and money came from certain German princes, but the plot was betrayed and Condé saved himself by allowing the guilt to fall upon a subordinate. Although a ruthless punishment was meted out to the conspirators, yet this year 1560 seems to mark the advent of a more lenient policy towards religious dissenters. The repressive policy of Henry II had not cured the dissidence in the church, but it had weakened the kingdom. The Edict of Ecouen had driven from the country many industrious workers; at the same time, the fold of the Huguenots was scarcely depleted, so great was the enthusiasm for conversion.[2] A system of consistent exile or slaughter would have threatened the kingdom with serious loss. It was probably as much practical governmental interest, as relaxation of persecuting zeal which led to the promulgation of the Edict of Amboise in March, 1560. While equivocally worded, nevertheless this decree improved the situation of dissenters, in that it granted an amnesty to those in custody, without definitely proclaiming freedom of worship. The intention seems to have been to give liberty of conscience without liberty of public assembly,—in other words, to maintain order without infringing upon the privacy of the individual mind. In another two months still further measures were taken; the disciplinary movement in the church, which had marked the early part of the century, be-

[1] Hauser, *op. cit.*, p. 217.

[2] Hotman, *Gasparis Colinii Castelloni . . . Vita* (s. l. 1575), p. 26.

gan to revive. The Edict of Romorantin (May, 1560) requiring residence of bishops and other prelates, made heresy justiciable solely by the ineffective clerical courts, while lay tribunals were to pass on public gatherings. Coligny's influence upon the Queen Mother was making itself apparent; she had adopted a waiting policy, hoping to conciliate the opposing noble families until her sons should be grown and strong enough to impose their will; even the Cardinal of Lorraine considered the interests of the kingdom would best be served by avoiding too great an insistence on conformity.[1] The Huguenots continued in their faith, and in their peculiar system of administration, setting it up as a sharp contrast to the constantly increasing autocracy of royal rule. That the epithet of heretic was in any sense applicable seemed to them incredible; they felt themselves purer in their faith, closer to the primitive Church, than any follower of Rome. They declined to be judged by the Council of Trent, to which they had been refused admittance, but professed an eagerness to discuss their cause before a national council of the French clergy. Meanwhile they lived in a precarious peace.

Restless dissatisfaction was seeking an outlet for expression. Reprints of the proceedings of the Estates of Tours appeared; men began to discuss the privileges and duties of the Estates General. In August the king's advisers yielded so far as to summon to Fontainebleau a group of the lords of church and state, to deliberate upon the difficulties of the realm. At this time Coligny ventured to lay before the king a petition signed by 50,000 Huguenots of Normandy, asking for the right of public worship, and relief from interference of judges of the Roman Catholic faith, who (they said) conducted themselves more like adherents of the Roman pontiff than equitable judges and teachers.[2] They renewed their

[1] L. Romier, *La Conjuration d'Amboise* (Paris, 1923), p. 207.

[2] Hotman, *Colinii . . . Vita*, p. 28; Romier, *La Conjuration*, p. 207.

request for a national council, and for the Estates General, supported in this latter respect by various Catholic speakers. Some declared it would be most advantageous to summon the public council of the realm; this course was recommended especially by "Marillac the Archbishop of Vienne and de l'Hôpital the Chancellor, ... who declared that the council was a very ancient institution of the Francs, which had continued in use until recent times but which had lapsed, on account of slanders".[1] It was decided to summon the Estates to Meaux in December; the question of the council was more difficult, because it was not advisable to erect a competitive body to that which the Pope had summoned,—and prorogued—at Trent. Since the negotiations with the Vatican failed to elicit any definite indication of the renewal of the general council, a resolution was finally taken to call a meeting of the French clericals in January 1561.

Thus the agitation resolved itself into a plea for two distinct and concrete objectives both based fundamentally upon the principle of self-government. It was implicitly, though often inarticulately, felt that the question of abuse of government could not in justice be settled by the governors; it was for the governed to decide where lay the evils and the remedies; in like manner, it was for the entire body of Christian believers, or at any rate for the leaders of each different group, to discuss and settle matters of faith, even as the primitive Church had done.

The lapse of seventy-six years had obliterated the memory of former meetings of the Estates. Even the procedure of election had been forgotten. A widespread enfranchisement of serfs had occurred meanwhile, adding largely to the number of rural voters, who took a more general share in this election than they ever had taken. Provinces that had formerly been represented by three nominees of their own Es-

[1] Hotman, *Colinii . . . Vita*, p. 30.

tates now sent to Meaux [1] deputies elected by a process involving several stages. The communal assemblies sent their deputy to meet corresponding members of the entire chatellénie; these, in their turn, sent a member to the chief town of the bailliage, where the final cahier was drawn up.[2] The alteration in method was another serious blow at the feudal organisation, which had outlived the feudal lords. By ignoring the provincial estates, and establishing a framework subsidiary to the government at Paris, the centralising tendency of the monarchy imposed itself more emphatically than ever.[3] Furthermore, by removing the privilege of nomination from the provincial estates, whose Tiers Etat was drawn chiefly from the urban bourgeoisie, the countryside was put on an equal footing with the towns, and opinions obtained more nearly representative of the entire nation.

The advice of the Estates was sought in the conduct of government, in so far as its religious policy was concerned. It was hoped in addition to obtain a substantial subsidy [4] for even with the most rigorous economy, the Cardinal of Lorraine found it impossible to carry on the ordinary processes of administration with the royal revenues so heavily mortgaged as he had found them. The death of the young king, Francis II, occurring before the deputies had convened, fundamentally altered the situation. The heir, Charles IX, was without question a minor; vague discussion about the power of the Estates suddenly became pertinent; here was a case where there was obvious reversion of authority to the people. A council of regency must be named, and for this the deputies

[1] The place of meeting was later changed to Orleans.

[2] This does not apply to Burgundy, Brittany and Languedoc, which maintained the old system.

[3] Babeau, "La représentation du Tiers État . . . au xvie siècle," *Revue Historique* XXI (1883) 91; Romier, *La Conjuration*, p. 262.

[4] Garnier, *Chartes de Communes . . . en Bourgogne* (Dijon, 1918), pp. 210-211.

must return to seek further instructions from their constituents.[1] But the court party was not willing to recognize these theoretical capacities, either to nominate the council, or to accept an imperative mandate. The Queen Mother took matters into her own hands, and by the exercise of her native astuteness, soon turned the situation to her advantage. The Guises were dismissed; Mary Stuart was sent home, de l'Hôpital took over the finances from the Cardinal, the King of Navarre was placated with the title of lieutenant-general of the kingdom, and Catherine remained in command, regent in fact, if not in name.

On December 13, 1560, one week after the death of Francis II, the deputies actually met at Orleans where they listened to an address by the Chancellor de l'Hôpital [2] and, still expostulating on the necessity for a council of regency, drew up the general cahier for each order. Royal officials broached the matter of the debt, which the deputies were horrified to learn amounted to 43,000,000 livres, divided among direct loans and the hypothecation of revenues. No instructions had been given by the electorate with regard to the grant of so large a sum; in fact, the voters had been so absorbed in the religious and political side of the struggle that the question of costs had hardly entered in. The Third Estate was particularly inclined to cavil at this matter. They refused to incur any financial responsibility and as this was the object for which they had been summoned in the first instance, permission was at length won to return to their homes to ask the opinion of the taxpayers. It was really a notable victory, for in it was involved the whole question of absolutism versus individual liberty. In granting to his people several months for discussion, the monarch partly acknowledged that they

[1] Romier, *Catholiques et Huguenots à la cour de Charles IX* (Paris, 1924), p. 31.

[2] de l'Hôpital, *Oeuvres* (Paris, 1824), vol. i, pp. 375-376.

were not taillable à merci. They were unfortunately too little skilled in political manipulation to profit by the fruits of their firm stand.

The time of reunion was August, 1561, the place, Pontoise. In order to minimise expense, it was decided to send only one representative of each order from each province. In the invening period two further edicts were promulgated, defining more sharply the status of the reformed religion. There was to be no heckling of either party by the other, no use of offensive epithets, no violation of the privacy of homes without a written order. Permission even was granted to fugitives to return, if they would live at home "catholiquement et sans scandale". These provisions were to have force only until the action of the national council, so that every effort was made to send thither formidable arguments and effective orators. The clericals gathered at Poissy while the other two orders were at Pontoise.

The agenda of the political assembly turned upon three chief heads: the formation of the council of regency, the pacification of religious troubles, and the liquidation of debts.[1] The nobility had come in a more imperious mood than at Orleans, and made even more daring demands for legitimate control of the State.[2] But before they would proceed to the discussion of financial measures, they insisted upon the publication of an edict founded upon the complaints presented at the former session. The need was so urgent that the court hastened to comply.[3] The changes introduced fall into several groups: ecclesiastical discipline, twenty-seven clauses; reform of the judiciary, sixty-one; financial, twenty-three;

[1] Abord, *La Réforme et la Ligue à Autun* (Paris-Autun, 1855), vol. i, p. 126.

[2] Romier, *Catholiques et Huguenots*, p. 181.

[3] *Recueil de Pièces Originales et Authentiques concernant la tenue des États Généraux* (Paris, 1789), vol. i, p. 296.

commercial, seven; police, four; and a few others.[1] There was no mention of heresy, but the criticisms unfavorable to regular and secular clergy were plainly bearing fruit.

To emphasise her good faith in the observance of the traditions of government, and to make the ordinance doubly solemn, the regent submitted it for registration by Parlement, which in ponderous legal fashion undertook the discussion article by article.[2] In four days, they had completed the first clause! Meanwhile the Estates were awaiting the publication of the entire one hundred and fifty clauses, before they would take under consideration a grant of funds vitally necessary to the administration. In addition, a vexing political problem was introduced. The Estates General and the Parlement were both theoretical checks upon the absolutism of the monarchy.[3] How far was the one, in its capacity of registrator, justified in blocking a bill drawn in compliance with the wishes of the other, in its capacity as representative of the nation? Both bodies drew their origin from the same source, the curia regis; their rivalry did not abate until Parlement was destroyed by the Revolution.

There is still in existence the cahier of the noblesse at the Estates of Pontoise,[4] which expresses what were then ultra radical views on the lawful field of action of political assemblies. They aimed at control of the advisory council, both for the present reign, and for any future minority, as well as at periodic meetings of the Estates under any circumstances. Their first request was the submission for their approval of a list of the proposed council, from which they

[1] See table in Picot, vol. ii, p. 292.

[2] A. de Ruble, *Antoine de Bourbon et Jeanne d'Albret* (Paris, 1885), vol. iii, p. 147.

[3] Picot, *op. cit.*, vol. ii, p. 59.

[4] Bibl. Nat. Ms. Fr. 3970 mentioned by P. Van Dyke, "The Estates of Pontoise", *English Historical Review* XXVIII (1913) 493.

eliminated the names of all ecclesiastics. They then asked that provision be made for the convocation of the Estates whenever the crown passed to an heir less than twenty years old. The responsibility for the summons should rest with the nearest princes of the blood, but if they should prove negligent, then each bailliage should elect three deputies to meet at the expiration of a given period, in the palace, at Paris, at twelve o'clock. Any one, not a prince of the blood, who might presume to govern in the interim, should be attainted of treason. (Seemingly, they were not entirely pleased with Catherine.) The Estates were to have control of war and peace, taxes and disbursements, and were to meet regularly every two years.[1] Finally, they asked that all persecution on account of religion should cease.

The Third Estate supported the nobility in most of these opinions; it made some further suggestions of its own. In the financial discussion, the restitution of all gifts over 10,000 livres, and a general revision of the accounts were advocated by both orders. They united also in an attack on the Church, whose vast possessions were an intense irritation to the heavily taxed bourgeoisie. In this assembly the concept of a salaried clergy, its lands confiscated, its serfs enfranchised, its courts abolished, dependent for its very livelihood upon the State [2] was first brought forward by a deputy from Burgundy, who later made an eloquent plea for religious toleration.

Although safeconducts were granted to Théodore de Bèze, Peter Martyr, and other exiles, nothing was gained by the doctrinal discussion at Poissy, for the Cardinal craftily intro-

[1] Van Dyke, *ibid.*

[2] According to Abord, *op. cit.*, vol. i, pp. 127 *et seq.*; Garnier, *op. cit.*, p. 211 states only complete alienation of goods, a practical equivalent. De Bèze, *Histoire ecclésiastique des églises réformées* (Antwerp, 1580), vol. i, bk. 4, p. 474, quoting Bretaigne's speech, says two-thirds of the goods of the clergy.

duced the topic of consubstantiation, which caused a rift between the Lutherans and Calvinists. The only definite action was in the field of finance. Fearful lest some of the threats of the Estates might be put into execution, the clergy made a large grant, relieving the immediate necessities of the court. They thereby weakened the position of the other deputies, whose bargaining power was no longer great enough to obtain results. The ambitious program of the Third Estate failed, but its main clause, civil liberty, religious toleration, and confiscation of clerical lands lingered in memory until the day of a more powerful assembly. The only influence still strong enought to exert any reforming tendency was that of the chancellor, de l'Hôpital. His political wisdom must rest on the three ordinances of Orleans (1561), Rousillon (1563), and Moulins (1566), which embodied as far as practicable the requests of the Estates General (1560) with the additional surety accorded by a personal tour of the provinces.[1] To him also must be credited the Edict of Toleration of January, 1562, that gave permission to Huguenots to worship outside walled towns, or to hold private assemblies in their own houses without fear or molestation.

However wise this policy might ultimately have proved, for the moment it stirred up the retaliatory anger of the Romanists. An encounter at Vassy, two months later, between the worshipping Calvinists and a body of horsemen led by the Duke of Guise resulted in bloodshed, and Condé recklessly rallied his men to arms (March, 1562). It was a mistake, for the reformed party was in a minority and was nevertheless winning toleration from the government. A few more years would have strengthened their position. Instead, a decade of dreary intermittent warfare resulted, punctuated here and there by treaties ambiguous in their terms, or mutually contradictory, and reaching its climax in the massacre of August, 1572.

[1] Picot, *op. cit.*, vol. ii, p. 67.

CHAPTER II

HOTMAN: THE THEORIES OF THE OPPOSITION

HARDLY had the Huguenots found a military leader in Condé, than they discovered a pamphleteer, a diplomatic agent, and a political theorist in Francis Hotman (1524-1590). He was seriously implicated in the Conspiracy of Amboise, and his hate of the Guises was shown in a virulent booklet entitled *Epistre envoyée au Tigre de la France* (1560). This was a bold paraphrase, somewhat elaborated, of the first oration against Catiline with which Hotman, as a Ciceronian scholar, was extremely familiar. It met with more attention than it merited, for the Cardinal, after hanging the bookseller, endeavored to destroy every copy, and nearly succeeded.[1]

The attempt of the reformed party to dislodge the Guises and replace them by one of their own faith had failed. If they were still to attain their ends by constitutional means, they must win over and strengthen some other factor in the government.[2] Anthony of Navarre had proved but a frail

[1] The only one that eluded him was found in 1834 on a second hand book stall in the provinces. It went first into private possession, but was later bought by the city of Paris for 1,400 francs. In the Spring of 1871, the librarian of the Hotel de Ville carried the book home to examine at his leisure; it was thus accidentally rescued a second time from oblivion.

[2] ... narrat quae cum rege Navarrae egerit ut eum ad virilem actionem excitaret, quod tamen minime successisse videtur, ita ut iam de aliis mediis circumspiciendum sit: et quidem de proximis regni comitiis cogitat quae regis pupilli tutelam constituere debent. From a letter of Morel to Calvin, s.l. 15 August, 1559, printed in *Joannis Calvini Opera Quae Supersunt Omnia* (Brunswick, 1877), vol. xvii, # 3096.

reed. He was uncertain equally of his faith [1] and of his politics. Occasionally he was heard arguing the cause of Catherine de Medici against his own claims. It was suspected that Navarrese interests appealed to him more closely than French, and that his policies were directed by his desire to regain from Spain certain Basque lands.

The other possibilities were the Council of State, the Parlement, and the Estates General. The first of these was dominated by the Romanist party, the second was Gallican, but Catholic. The Huguenots decided that their hopes lay with the third. After the first civil war, Hotman published his *Antitribonian* (1567), primarily an attack on the teaching of Roman Law in French Universities, but containing in its final chapter a critical estimate of the weaknesses of Parlement. *Franco-Gallia,* his constructive work on the genesis and functions of the Estates, did not appear until a year after the massacre of St. Bartholomew. In so far as he made it a plea for kingship only by consent of the people his enemies were able, in later years, and under changed conditions, to refute his party with his own arguments. The death of the king's brother in 1584 brought the Protestant line of Navarre into the position of heirs presumptive,—a situation which scandalised the Romanists, who were then perfectly ready to accept the principle of an elective monarchy in order to exclude a heretic from the throne. At the request of Henry of Navarre, Hotman retraced his steps and produced *De Jure Successionis* (1585), supporting primogeniture, with reversion, if necessary, to the nearest male agnate. These three

[1] . . . . omniumque mortalium spem Navarrus miserrime fefellit. Si scires quam acriter sit admonitus, quae conditiones illi oblatae sint, quanta subsidia delata, quanta tamen inertia omnia despexerit, vehementer mirareris. Ego totos hosce menses duos numquam quievi. Sed video nos inaniter laborare. Hotman to Bullinger, Strassburg, 2 September, 1559, *Calvini Opera . . .*, vol. xvii, # 3108. See also Ruble, vol. iii, p. 33 for reference to Hotman's letter to the King of Navarre.

books resume the gist of his thoughts on French constitutional custom, although the complete list of his works contains about forty titles.

The personality of their author is preserved to us by his many letters, both published and manuscript. We have also two portraits; the death mask in Read's edition of Le Tigre,[1] bearing the legend

Rectius ut Juris nodos evolvere posses
Te magis Historiae nemo peritus erat,

and another in Ehinger,[2] taken from a painting in the aula of the University at Basel. This latter shows a man long-headed, thinfaced, the chin strong and pointed, a forehead possibly too lofty for harmony, fine aristocratic features, eyes well set,—the countenance of a man of keen perceptions, a trifle over-sensitive. We can learn from his letters of a quick temper, even of frequent quarrels, but there are the compensating factors of life-long friendships.

Born at Paris, the year before Pavia, of a family originally German,[3] the young Hotman lacked none of fortune's gifts. His father held a lucrative post in Parlement, which brought him in contact with the court and allowed him to maintain a small estate. The eldest son had all the advantages of education thrust upon him, and made sufficient use thereof to become instructor at the age of twenty-two in the law schools of Paris. Etienne Pasquier in his old age recalled that one of the most splendid opportunities of his youth was the day after Assumption, 1546, when he went to hear Hotman give his first lecture at the Écoles du Decret.[4]

[1] Reproduced from an earlier work of Boissardus, *Icones virorum illustrium* (Frankfort, 1597-1599), vol. iii, no. 28.

[2] *Historische Gesellschaft für Vaterländische Geschichte, Beiträge*, Neue Folge, Bd. IV, Heft I (Basel, 1892), frontispiece.

[3] Letter of Hotman to Bullinger, s. l. 12 April, 1558, Paris, Bibl. Nat., Fonds Latin, 8586.

[4] Pasquier, *Lettres* (Paris, 1619), vol. ii, p. 501.

A year had not passed before the young instructor stealthily departed from his father's house and made his way to Lyons. It was the end of the reign of Francis I; Calvin had published the final edition of his Confession; a few martyrs had suffered for their faith in Paris; discussion and agitation were rife. Hotman moved in a circle of humanists and philosophers drawn from all Europe; he came in contact with the more daring minds which had questioned the authority of the Middle Age; he too underwent a spiritual change,[1] and forswore the Church of Rome. For this his father disowned him, and pursued him with threats of violence. We find a letter of Hotman's addressed to Calvin from Lyons, July, 1548, " . . . . But whither then shall I go? Do you think that I am pleased with this city, in which I can hardly enter . . . . an inn without fearing to encounter some one of my father's friends coming to find me?" And again to Melanchthon, "If I had remained there [in Paris] any longer, his impious hands could not have been kept from me."[2] His uneasiness in this regard, and his loneliness made him yearn to escape to Geneva.

I call to God to witness that not even my father ever was regarded with such great love and piety as you are surrounded, from whom I learned to think piously. . . . Nothing more pleasant could happen than if [God] himself should grant some opportunity of living near you. . . . If I had twenty pieces of gold. . . . I should most gladly spend the winter near you, if you would permit.[3] . . . . Oh that we might use, not these written words, but actual speech. . . . Now that so many of our

[1] Possibly through direct contact with Calvin: see letter of 27 July, 1548, *infra*.

[2] Hotman to Melanchthon, Strassburg, 24 May, s. a. [1555?] Bibl. Nat., Coll. Dupuy 729, folio 212.

[3] Hotman to Calvin, Lyons, 27 July, 1548, *Calvini Opera*... vol. xiii, # 1056.

people have gone off to you. . . . I am left alone, nor do I know what I am to do.[1]

He utilized the enforced leisure in the compilation of a treatise, *De Actionibus,* the manuscript of which was sent in October for Calvin's approval. By some means he succeeded in reaching Geneva, probably in the early winter of 1548, and after a brief service as one of Calvin's secretaries, departed to take up teaching at Lausanne. It is rather disappointing to find in his letters of this period, when he had actually escaped persecution and attained means of earning a slender livelihood, a querulous restlessness and self-pity which he could well have spared his correspondents, even if they existed within him. He found the work exhausting, and too elementary to be worthy of his attention, he was without friends, he was underpaid, hopes of winning his inheritance were dim.[2] Despite all these drawbacks, he married. We have no expression of Calvin on this step, but we have clear testimony that he did not approve the constant desire for change. There are replies from Hotman, somewhat apologetic, in which he denies that he has ever seriously considered such a move, but in the autumn of 1555 we find him in Strassburg. His father had died; there was again the question of obtaining his patrimony, and an exile in the Empire would be held in better favor than one from Calvinistic Lausanne.[3] Until this time, his intellectual labors had been in the classical field.

1 H. to Calvin, Lyons 27 August, 1548, *ibid.*, # 1067.

2 Hotman to Calvin, Lausanne, 12 July, 1552, in *Cal. Opera*, vol. xiv, # 1638 and # 1649 (6 Sept.). But compare Viretus to Calvin, Lausanne, 12 February, 1550, where he says "Hottomanus admissus est a senatu Bernensi, cum stipendio satis iusto, ad moderandam primam classem. Habet in singulos menses coronatos tres et tritici mensuram quam cuppam vocant. Nullus antehac in ea functione tanto donatus est stipendio." *Cal. Opera*, vol. xiii, # 1343.

3 H. to Melanchthon, "parenti meo venerando", Strassburg, 24 May, s. a. [1556?] Bibl. Nat., Coll. Dupuy, no. 729, fol. 212.

He had lectured on Roman Law; he had traced the development of Roman constitutional history, and whatever of public life he could discover in the works of Cicero and Caesar. His mind, then, was steeped in the ancient world. So far as the actual political environment had affected his spiritual growth, the influence had been rather numbing than stimulating. Now, when just turned thirty, he found himself cast into the thick of political discussion, both practical and theoretic.

As an imperial city, holding immediately from Charles V, Strassburg had been spared the necessity of accepting the faith of any Prince. Its citizens were mostly Lutheran, but tolerant enough to make their home the gathering place of refugees from many lands. Those whom the Peace of Augsburg had forced to choose between home and faith, and those who could not assent to the severity of Geneva, those who had fled from the Marian persecution of 1553-1558,—a sprinkling of all found their way to Strassburg. In Hotman's letters of this period we find reference to various English friends [1] and there are also dedications addressed to them.

He was pleased with his new home, and with the audience which greeted his lectures.

> The eagerness of the students is incredible not only for the study of law, but even for so humble a speaker [Homuncionem]. . . . I am grieved that I am unable to satisfy the zeal of these men, who declare that more than twenty have come for the express purpose of hearing us. . . . But if I start private work, they tell me that I shall violate the statutes of the school, which forbid private lectures.[2]

Elsewhere he adds: " About forty students have presented a

[1] Hotman to Calvin, Strassburg, 25 March, 1556, *Cal. Opera* XVI, # 2416; 24 October, 1556, *ibid.*, # 2546.

[2] H. to Boniface Amerbach, Strassburg, 20 January, 1555/6, Basel, Öffentliche Bibliothek, G II 19, folio 112-113.

petition . . . . that they might enjoy the hope which has brought them here—no less than that they might hear unworthy me. Never did I think that my little books could instill so great a devotion to me among scholars." [1]

The enthusiasm for his lectures stirred him to greater endeavor. In February he wrote to Herwagen and Son, printers at Basel, (a city through which he had passed on the journey from Lausanne) thanking them for a volume of Plutarch's Lives, and asking for the Ethics and Politics of Aristotle—in Latin; likewise the most recent edition of Demosthenes,—also in Latin, and Plautus with notes. He added a request that any moneys not expended should be returned promptly, because he had been put to great expense in a recent purchase of books, which included the works of the legists Bartolus, Alexander, Paul and Baldus.[2] He was engaged at the same time in private research, for in the summer he wrote to Bullinger at Zurich, " In your public library there is an old manuscript of the *Institutes,* without a gloss; to this added, if I remember correctly, a treatise *De Regulis Juris.* A long time ago I told Gesner that these *Institutes* were essential to my work." [3] Returning from a trip to Frankfort with Calvin, he received Bullinger's reply—" I have found at home two things which please me exceedingly, your letter, and the Institutes which I have been so eagerly awaiting . . . . I will compare [them] . . . . as quickly as possible with my text, and God willing will return them to you safely." [4] To another friend, Boniface Amerbach of Basel, he confided news of his intended work. " Before long I

[1] To Boniface Amerbach, Strassburg, 8 October, 1555 [1556?], Basel, G II 19, fol. 114.

[2] To Herwagen, Strassburg, 17 February, 1556, Basel, Fr. Gr. Ms. II 2, fol. 84.

[3] To Bullinger, s. l. 8 July, 1556, Bibl. Nat., Fonds Latin, 8586.

[4] H. to Bullinger, Strassburg, 22 Sept., 1556, *Cal. Opera,* vol. xvi, # 2539.

hope to publish a little book, *De Optimo Genere Iuris Interpretandi.* In this you will observe my custom of interpretation, which I have drawn, not from the turbid lacunae of our own rhetoricians, but from the purest fonts of antiquity." [1] And later

As far as my studies are concerned, I have finished the book, *De Optimo Genere,* but I will polish it off at my leisure. I cannot remember ever having been so happily engaged. The *Pandects* with my notes are now being published at Lyons. . . . I am completing the commentaries on the *Institute* from my lectures. . . . I hope that I shall make an end of it before Easter. Since I happened upon an ancient codex from the Senate at Zurich, I have restored the text. Wherever I could, I have affixed to the separate paragraphs a Latin heading, indicating the Law of the Digest or Codex whence they were drawn. The material I have divided into "enunciations", to each of which I have joined its own laws and authorities; and in almost every case I have added a statement of that interpretation which I now follow.[2]

He seems to have had the usual difficulties with the printer, for a year later he writes to Herwagen and Brand (typographers at Basel) inquiring anxiously about the non-appearance of the book.[3]

He continued happy in his new home, though there were

[1] Strassburg, 12 June, 1557, Basel, G II 19, fols. 222, 223.

[2] H. to Amerbach, Strassburg, 28 August, 1557, Basel, G II 19, fols. 224-225.

[3] Strassburg, 5 August, 1558, Basel, Fr. Gr. Ms. II 27 No. 136. In a letter to Amerbach of the following November, he exclaims with characteristic impatience "... neque scio, ita me amet Deus, utrum viri an mortui sint... Quid causa sit, quod cum vicies, ut opinor, ad D. Herwagium et ipsum his tribus mensibus scripserim, tamen multis precibus literatam unam extorquere [non] potui."

When it actually did appear in the Spring of 1559, he comments to Herwagen, "Deus bone! Quibus typis es usus! Pulcherrimi sunt, sed minutiss." Fr. Gr. Ms. II 27, # 125.

rumors of his difficult temper and too vivid imagination. "Never have my private affairs been in a better state, thank God. Our school of civil law flourishes so notably that I am in the good graces of our Senate on this account. If only there were some definite system, I should adjudge myself fortunate and even blest." [1] He was absorbed in the work and the students; he wrote at length to Amerbach on the new method which he was developing, and its superiority to that of former schools.[2] Young men from Poland and Vienna took the long journey to hear him lecture; his former friend Sir Thomas Wrothe, who had returned to England in 1558, sent his eldest son to be trained in civil law.[3]

But from this life of eager activity, brimful of the pursuits of peace, he was called to more dangerous tasks. Henry II had died in July, 1559. In March followed the attempt of Condé to obtain possession of the young king at Amboise. In this conspiracy Hotman may have been involved; shortly after, his venomous attack on the Cardinal was printed. There seems a little doubt that so hotheaded an enthusiast would gladly have joined in such a plot, although his share was confined chiefly to an injudicious and premature babbling. During the following summer, he set off for Nérac, to execute a delicate diplomatic mission at the court of Anthony

[1] To Bullinger, s. l. 11 January, 1557, *Cal. Opera*, vol. xvi, # 2580.

[2] "Quod tamen non eo dico, ut Deus testis est, quo plus aliis me vidisse glorier." s.l. 1 June, 1559, Basel, G II 19, fol. 141.

[3] *Cal. Opera*, vol. xvii, # 3032. This young man probably followed the same regime as that ordered by Hotman for the son of his friend Stuckius, a clergyman at Zurich—"Dedimus illi lectulum in cubiculo proximo, more Gallico exornatum. Hora VI suasi ut Biblia legeret, et precaretur. Septima me audit; et videtur affici voluptate audiendi rationem Reip. Rom. Octava Philippicas Demosth. et prima partitiones et Quarta impetravi a paedigogo quodam Anglorum ut ei liceret audire Dialecticam una cum suis preciis. Denique spero ipsum otiosum apud me non futurum." To Bullinger, s. l. 15 May, 1559, Bibl. Nat., Fonds Latin 8586, printed in *Epistolae ... F. et J. Hotomannorum* (Amsterdam, 1700).

of Navarre. Although this has remained obscure, it probably was inspired by the hope of converting the king to Calvinism. At all events it failed, for Hotman wrote to Bullinger "The king . . . . has satisfied no one, not even us". He returned to Strassburg, but his letters reflect the altered character of his life. There is little about the students or the lectures, much about conditions, religious and political, in France and in Central Europe. He was in touch with the evangelical princes of Germany; he sent to the king of Navarre a careful account of the European situation, with a view to possible allies, mentioning also their hopes that His Majesty would have more regard to the obedience which he owed to God than to the friendship of tyrants who are held in execration by God and man.[1]

In March, 1562, Parlement under protest accepted the Edict of Toleration, granting to Calvinists the right to meet outside walled towns. This partial alleviation of repression inspired Hotman, restless as ever, to return to his native land. The following month he wrote to Amerbach from Orleans "I am sending you the story of the slaughter committed by the Guise party at Vassy, on the first of March. This I have translated into Latin from the little sheets in the vernacular which . . . are passed about."[2] Almost at the same time he wrote to the Elector Palatine[3] and to Sir William Cecil,[4] bemoaning the calamitous state of the kingdom. He made some flying trips back to Strassburg ("being in this town for the affairs of M. le prince de Condé") on diplomatic business, but the vacillation of his chiefs disheartened him.

[1] From Strassburg, 31 December, 1560, printed by Hauser in *La Revue Historique*, XIX (1891), 54.

[2] H. to Amerbach, Orleans, 12 April, 1562, Basel, G II 19, fol. 148.

[3] Kortuem, J. F. C., *Nonnullae Hotomanni Epistolae* (Heidelberg, 1844).

[4] British Museum, Additional Mss. 4160, printed in *La Revue Historique*, II (1876), 35.

"Je me suis esbahy comment le roi de Navarre a voulu mander aux predicans d'Orléans qu'il recognoissoit a faulte . . . . Cependant je n'ose dire qu'il participast au bon tour qu'on a voulu jouer à son frère, qui est ung vray mouton." [1] By the end of the year, we find him at Valence, once more enmeshed in the routine of university life.

I have come hither with this hope, that by my own industry I might restore this school, which has been neglected, and almost totally destroyed. But we shall have to turn aside a little from our usual custom, and adapt ourselves to this audience, which is accustomed to the disputations of the Bartolists. . . . We are not so much occupied in interpreting the civil law, as in cleaning the Augean stables, as it were. . . . Our zeal, and all the activities of the students are remarkably favored by our bishop, whose benevolence towards me and mine increases each day.[2]

His appointment to the chair at Valence was due to the influence of this same bishop, Monluc, suspected by the court of motives too kindly towards the Huguenots. After four years of service, a more advantageous offer from the king's aunt called him to the University of Bourges in the Spring of 1567. His journeyings to and fro had brought him into contact with Coligny,[3] and he seems to have come under the sway of Michel de l'Hôpital during this same period.[4] In

[1] H. to the Elector Palatine 11 July, 1562. Printed in *La Revue Hist.*, II (1876), 37.

[2] H. to de Mesmes, Valence, December, 1563 and April, 1566, printed in *La Revue Historique de Droit français et étranger*, I (1855), 194. Originals at the Bibl. Nat.

[3] Visited him at Chatillon, 3 October, 1563. See his letter to the Duke of Würtemberg, in the *Revue Historique*, II (1876), 45.

[4] See the preface dedicated to de l'Hôpital from Valence 6 Kal. Jan. 1563/4, in *Hotomanni Opera*, vol. iii, p. 25, internal evidence in *Antitribonian*, and the preface to the Duchess of Bourges in the *Opera*, vol. iii, p. 29, dated Aureliae X Kal. Aug. MDLXIIX (sic) "tibi studium observantiam ac pietatem debeam: tum vero hanc ob causam vel maxime, quod me tibi a Michaele Hospitalio Franciae nostrae Cancellario, hoc est ... altero Solone oblatum, in illam tuam Academiam adscivisti ..."

the book which he produced towards the end of the year, he was to some extent the mouthpiece of the Chancellor, although he represents also the views of Carolus Molinaeus, in whose home he had worked as a young attorney, twenty years before. De l'Hôpital was anxious to untangle the difficulties in the legal situation by codifying the law. A start had been made in the codification of customs in the reign of Charles VII, which had been followed up rather half-heartedly by later monarchs. Louis XII had even ordered an extensive tour of the kingdom, to obtain information requisite for the task.[1]

The fundamental problem was the contradiction between the Roman Code and the Teutonic customs, both simultaneously extant in France. Feudal law had prevailed in the north and west since the sixth century; Roman law had crept up from the old Provincia until in the thirteenth century it disputed the field, and made ambiguous the national jurisprudence. Although Hotman had taught it at Valence, Bourges and Orleans, and even in Paris itself under peculiar circumstances, nevertheless he was not in sympathy with that subtle hairsplitting necessitated by the application of an ancient code to the conditions of the contemporary world. We have seen that he complained of the Bartolists and the Augean stables at Valence. Bartolus had but tried to reconcile the clauses of the Code, and the interpretations of the Digest, with conditions in fourteenth century Italy. His northern followers were trying to apply them to a land not native to them, a land nurtured on Teutonic law for an interval of seven hundred years.

The tradition of absolutism pervading the Code was another danger which threatened France. The south had kept its

[1] Molinaeus, *Coustumes de la Prévosté et Vicomté de Paris* (Paris, 1691), vol. ii, p. 30. Babeau, "La Représentation du Tiers État... au xvie siècle", *Revue Historique*, XXI (1893), 92-93.

Roman law after Rome itself had fallen; there remained the municipia, the consuls (as local officials) and the panoply of Roman provincial life, reduced indeed to a ghost that walked by day, but which could not fail to suggest the centralisation of the past, the supreme authority of a being whose very wish had the force of law. If the Code were allowed to supersede the customaries, if the jurisprudence which centered its philosophy around the existence of an omnipotent legislator and executive were to supplant a jurisprudence which, however primitive and forest-born, assumed the existence and co-operation of a representative body, then the French monarch would tread that path to absolutism which the Huguenots were loathe to see him take.

It was with this two-fold purpose,—one practical, immediate, adjusting the tools to the demands of the age,—the other vague, but no less real, warding off the potential danger which threatened a bourgeoisie awake to its political needs,—that Hotman must have written *Antitribonian*.

He makes a direct attack at the outset, marking the impropriety of twisting the State into conformity with a foreign law, ridiculing the reverence paid to the Code, mocking its lack of practical utility—" Let some one ", says he, " equipped with this knowledge alone come into any court of the realm: who does not know that he would be as strange and bewildered as if he had come into the new world, and the solitudes of America." [1] And again,

To which of two studies ought a young man apply himself: should he learn the Roman and Constantinopolitan magistrates, or should he learn the officials of the crown, and of the court trials of this kingdom? . . . Should he know the royal prerogatives, the power and authority of the three estates, the rights of the queen, of the Dauphin, of the king's brothers. . . . ? [2]

[1] Hotman, *Antitribonian* (Leipsig, 1734), p. 51.

[2] *Ibid.*, p. 48.

He contrasts the social world in which they live with that of the Romans.

> With us, we have first general distinction, that some are nobles and some plebs. Each type has its own law. . . . Then we have this further division, that some are lords of a fief, others vassals; let us add the chatelain, and those who have pure and mixed justice. . . . There is a third classification, of those who are free, or of those who are serfs. Furthermore the servile condition. . . . is attributed to some because they are taxable-at-will, others pay a definite sum, others are mainmorts, others have not the freedom of contracting marriage. . . . The learned of every age have agreed. . . . that the laws ought to be adapted to the state and form of a polity, not the polity to the laws.[1]

His ostensible purpose is a treatise on education, for says he " since I sometimes hesitate and distrust the system under which a large share of the youths of France are trained, I have yielded to the temptation of declaring my opinion, as modestly and as gently as possible." He did not adhere very strictly to the latter part of his program, for his opinions and emotions were always closely involved, so that he found it difficult not to be carried away by his arguments, not to put all his energy into the matter in hand. Philosophic detachment was not for him.

He considers as axiomatic the statement " It is useless to study an art which has no practical application ". Granting that one should study only what is useful, and that it is difficult to retain in mind what has been learned, without daily exercise thereof, he devotes a chapter each to the various topics of the civil law—the law of persons, the nature of things, inheritance, agency, contracts, litigation,—in order to show their complete inapplicability to sixteenth century France. The ancients were wiser than this; they taught their

[1] Hotman, *op. cit.*, pp. 51 and 40.

young men by constant attendance in the law courts. It is interesting to note this frank declaration of utilitarianism, for his next important work bases its thesis upon the claims of precedent.

If any one would plead that, while it is evident that the student of Roman law can not practice this in France, nevertheless his studies are not wasted, for the law gives a picture of Roman life, and so illuminates his knowledge of history, Hotman would retort

Who does not know that, so far as Roman magistrates are concerned, more can be learned in one year from the reading of Greek and Latin histories and that far more pleasantly and easily than in six years from those fragments and patches which compose the books of Justinian?. . . . There are no young men more ignorant of history, be it foreign or French, than those who return from the Universities. . . . It is certain that from one book of Livy, Suetonius or Tacitus more is understood, than from five great volumes of Justinian and with a thousand times greater pleasure and profit.

To prove this he traces the history of the Code from the time of its promulgation in the sixth century until its partial reception in France in the thirteenth.

In the first place, he is dissatisfied with the accomplishment of Tribonian and his assistants. It was not a consistent piece of work at the start. Then

these books, although they were written in Latin, nevertheless remained in Greece, where they were read in the schools of Constantinople. . . . The emperors altered the text of Justinian in whatsoever respect it pleased them. . . . They were printed [excussae] in Greek type, and given to the public in twelve or fifteen years. Meanwhile Italy, having been conquered by northern races, took over their laws and statutes, and for the space of six hundred years knew little or nothing of the books of Justinian. For the laws of the Goths, Vandals and Franks lasted until the times of Lothaire the Saxon, who became emperor about the year 1125. . . . Historians report that in the time of this Lothair, there lived a man of great name and authority, Irnerius or Werner, concerning whom the history by the Abbot of Ursperg thus speaks: " At the same time D. Werner at the request of the Countess Matilda brought forward the books of the law which now for a long time had been neglected."

He mentions the work of Gratian in compiling the canon law into a form similar to that of the civil code, for which he assigns the rather late date 1150, and recognises its importance in the spread of the Code.

In this way foreign princes, who wished to endow their states with schools, were forced, on account of the fusion, to receive the training in the canon law also. . . . The system of Justinian's books was adjusted to the might of the Roman chair. *For the one clings to the other,* as a necessary appendix. Thence came that stupid custom, which not so long ago held in France, that all acts and public instruments must be written in Latin.

The first part of the accusation may perhaps be granted. Gibbon calls the work of Tribonian a " Tessellated pavement of antique and costly, but too often of incoherent, fragments ". He tries to defend it on the ground that the ministers of Justinian, although they quoted only three names of the republican era, nevertheless were justified, for they " were instructed to labor, not for the curiosity of antiquarians, but for the immediate benefit of his subjects ". In adopting this line of defense, Gibbon unconsciously strengthened the claim of Hotman (whom he accuses of " passionate charges "), that the Code and Pandects were not a trustworthy source for information on the Roman life of any other era than the sixth century A.D.

The later passages of Hotman's narrative seem to indicate

an ignorance of that system known as the personality of law, which prevailed in France and Italy after the influx of the barbarians, and which invariably permitted every official of the Roman Church to be judged by Roman law, though it may have been by the code of Theodosius rather than by that of Justinian. Modern legal historians are inclined to believe that the great code never completely disappeared from the Romagna, or from that portion of the peninsula which remained the longest under Greek rule. Hotman perhaps allows himself a loophole in his " aut nullum aut exiguum ", but the chief stress of his argument is upon the break in continuity.

Similarly he claims that Roman law disappeared for a long time from France.

> The kingdom of Gaul through the grace of God flourished for eight hundred years, though it made little of the books of Justinian, and did not apply them. For it is not more than three hundred years [he was writing in 1567] that the practice of this study in France has been known, nor did Doctors of this profession cross the Alps until a long time after the instauration of Irnerius. . . . Although on account of the control of the Romans, certain traces of their law seem to have remained even for some time after the Franks had seized the kingdom,

nevertheless it waned. St. Louis did not apply a foreign code, when he sat under the oak at Vincennes; Honorius III had forbidden it to the University of Paris, and Philip Augustus had confirmed the decree. Roman law was not used in 1294 when Philip the Long [sic] convoked a Parlement at Paris, composed of prelates, barons, knights and plebs, of whom some could barely read. Customary law must have been applied then. So far as France is concerned, modern knowledge apparently confirms Hotman,[1] although the period of non-recognition has been shortened.

[1] *Cf. Cambridge Medieval History*, vol. iv, pp. 748-749.

He cannot be too scathing about the glosses.

Justinian himself, if he were to return, would not recognize his own work, nay, he might even repudiate it as the work of another. Meanwhile we can judge from these facts, how great is the good fortune of our young men, who spend the best part of their lives in the study of these books, of which the greatest part has been abrogated, or is full of confusion and contradiction, or marred by flaws and errors, brought into doubt and controversy through the corrections and changes which have been made in abundance.

The net result to sixteenth century France has been endless litigation. The lawyers dispute as to technicalities; they are interested not in justice, but in profits; they seek not a decision, but delay; Parlement does not aid the nation, it impedes it, and all through the influence of an antiquated and unreliable compilation.[1]

In his constructive suggestions, he embodies a philosophy of slow growth and change, retaining the best of the old, adding to this the lessons of more recent experience, with something of foresight and plan for the future,—a program that would not have shocked Edmund Burke too greatly.

It would be helpful. . . . especially at this time, when it has pleased God to grant to our France this Solon (I mean the great Michel de l'Hôpital), to summon several jurisconsults, together with learned statesmen, and an equal number of barristers and solicitors, and to enjoin them, that they should condense into one book whatever they may select and excerpt from the books of Justinian, as well as from the experience which they have gleaned from practice. . . . It would be worthy of Christian lawgivers to cull from the law of Moses, not those special enactments which concern the polity of the Jewish Republic, but those which are founded on justice, reason and natural equity, to

[1] Note: It is well to bear in mind that Hotman had for some years been trying to obtain the restitution of his paternal inheritance.

which all men, both those who preceded, and those who follow Moses, were, are, and shall be, subjected.[1]

It is significant of the increasing interest in national literature that Hotman wished this compilation to be written in French —" langage vulgaire et intelligible ",—not only the portion covering private law, but also that which concerned affairs of State. Where it seemed wise, they should follow the order of Justinian, but above all, they should fit the whole to the type and form of the French State.

He was willing to grant something to human weakness— " ce désir naturel que nous avons d'apprendre et [de] discourir "—but this communicative urge should not spend itself in froth, but rather in matters of profit to human life. There is an infinite number of questions " fondées sur une equité naturelle et plus dignes d'exercer les esprits des hommes, que celles qui ne sont fondées que sur petits fatras de lettres et de syllabes, et communément sur un pied de mouche ".

From the codification of law he returned to the topic whence he started—the education of French youths. Until the age of twenty they should occupy themselves with literature, human knowledge, and above all with moral philosophy; they should then pass on to the university for a period of two years, where they should hear discussions on equity, and obtain some practical experience. By this means they would have leisure to turn occasionally to another interest, such as the Holy Scriptures, philosophy, and history; they might thereby make the end and aim of their existence, not the multiplication of cases, but peace, concord and tranquillity in the nation.

The book ends on that note—tranquillity—and perhaps the author was beginning to feel its need. In the space of twenty years he had been the puppet of fortune, which had forced

[1] *Antitribonian* (Paris, 1616), p. 109.

him to play many roles. He had been a scholar at twenty-three, a practising attorney, a religious convert, in full flight before an irate parent; then a teacher, an author, a man of action, unsuccessful in his diplomatic work, returning with some trepidation to his native land, when the tempest seemed to abate. At the age of forty-three he had known something of the world, had tasted of its bitterness, was perhaps glad to settle down to the quiet of a provincial town, where he could reflect upon what had been, and what was to come. His philosophy in middle years demanded depth of learning, breadth of view, a practical turn in its application, simplicity and peace. That, to him, was the good life.

But peace he was not to have. The second civil war broke out in September 1567. As a Protestant, with a German name, he was at once an object of suspicion and attack. His home was pillaged and burnt; he fled to de l'Hôpital, in Paris, and then went on to Orleans. In the autumn of 1568, still a third war devastated France. Orleans proved unsafe, so he took his family to a small town near Sancerre. Here with the two books which remained to him,—the Bible and St. Augustine—, he composed the *Consolatio e Sacris Litteris.* Even in this obscure retreat he was not safe. The preface to a later edition of the *Consolatio* depicts the plight of his family:

Voici bientôt quarante ans que je ne cesse d'être le jouet de la fortune, agité et ballotté sans repos, mais je ne me souviens pas d'avoir jamais plus souffert que le jour où, arraché par miracle aux mains sanglantes de nos ennemis, après le pillage de mes meubles et de mes livres, chargé de sept enfants, manquant de tout et comme naufragé, au moment même où je croyois avoir trouvé un asile dans une petite ville à peine fortifiée, j'appris que nous y serions bientôt assiégés.[1]

His wife and new-born child nearly died at this time.

[1] Hotman, *Opera,* vol. iii, p. 154.

But fate had even worse in store—it had the night of St. Bartholomew. From the horrors of that massacre he fled across the frontier into Switzerland, with the vow never again to set foot in France.

Three days since did I arrive here, having escaped from a most appalling catastrophe, such a one as I do not think has occurred in God's Church since the creation. Fifty thousand men were slaughtered in the space of eight days. The rest wander about in the woods or, lying in prison, await the hands of their murderers. I assure you that by far the greatest part of the Papists are alienated from the King on this account, and detest these plots and this treachery. The country folk, harassed by lack of supplies, openly assert that they are ready to leave the home of their forefathers and to wander forth to other lands. So I can only marvel, if indeed what I heard on the way is true, that your neighbors and allies have decided to send new forces to the King, although even the French papist nobility itself openly and clearly refuses the King its aid in this cause, partly on account of the unspeakable and unheard-of perfidy which has stained the reputation of the French race, partly on account of the horrible suffering and agitation of their families. For there is not an illustrious house which was not affected by this slaughter. . . . So it is certain that the authors of these calamities, when they shall have been advised about the complaints of the nobility and the people, will regret deeply, but too late.[1]

In order to obtain assistance for the Huguenots from the

[1] Hotman to Gualter, Geneva, 4 October, 1572, printed in the *Revue Historique de Droit français et étranger*, I (1855), 496. The original is at Zurich. He goes on to say "Praevotius noster ad quem scribebas Lutetiae in aedibus comitum Rupifocaldii interfectus est; non procul secundus meus filius, quem D. Martyr in baptismo Theager nominarat; uxor mea raptata, multis contumeliis vexata; bona nostra omnia direpta sunt. Numquam puto Sathanae furias tantam in homines pios vim habuisse. Spero vos fratres et consanguineos aerumnas nostras miserari, et earum non modo in precibus vestris, verum etiam in concionibus meminisse, et hanc causam magistratibus vestris assidue commendare.

German princes, he planned to publish the tale of the massacre, which his friends in Switzerland were to spread abroad. "You ask me for the story of the massacres in France . . . . It shall be written in French and Latin, and we should advise you, as well as the people of Heidelberg, to arrange for a German translation." [1] His patriotism did not scruple at the introduction of foreigners into his native land, whether they were German mercenaries [2] or English sailors. An attempt to raise the English colors in the South-west did not shock him, for faith was his highest allegiance. A letter of the following December betrays this:

We have received letters from some papists of Lyons who tell us that the people of La Rochelle have torn down the royal banners everywhere, and demanded their former independence. . . . They see that every town in France which has received a garrison is reeking with blood, full of orphans and beggar children. They see that good faith and sworn vows count for nothing . . . . that all the laws and institutions of the kingdom, which are the foundations of the State, are abrogated by tyrannical acts. . . . I do not see any justice in blaming the deed of the Rochellois when at the same time they praise the bravery of the Swiss, because they claimed their independence. . . . Rumor has it that the Rochellois are thinking of allying themselves, or

[1] H. to Bullinger, Geneva, 10 October, 1572, published by R. Dareste in *Rev. Historique*, II (1876), 56.

[2] H. to Landgraf Philipp von Hessen, June 7, 1562. "Es begeren die Stende zu Orlianz, das E. S. Gn. durch die Barmherzigheit Gottes inen zu ehister Zeit welle... Reutter zu Hilff schicken und dieselbigen ezliche Monat besolden, dergestalt dass Ew. s. Gn. alles Geld, so hiezu aufgewendet getreulich widdergegeben werde, derfür sie, die Stende, Ew. s. Gn. alle Ire Gütter, beweglich und unbeweglich verpfenden. Die Stende begeren sollichs so hefftig und empsig dass sie auch mehr nicht thun konnten—sie versehen sich auch, ess werde der aller Christlichste König und seine Frau Mutter die Konigin Ew. s. Gn. darfür sich dankbarlich erzeigenn." Printed in Ehinger, "Franz Hotman", *Historische Gesellschaft ... Beiträge*, p. 92.

rather of giving themselves, to the English. If you could write to England in their favor, I believe that you would render a great service to our unhappy brothers.[1]

The idea of a betrayal of trust constantly returned. In the last two letters he mentioned fundamental laws, "institutions which are the foundation of the State", and their abrogation by tyranny. The juxtaposition of these two concepts drove him into the ranks of the contractualists. Even so early as 1567, he had referred to the power and authority of the three estates; he had followed with interest the course of events in the only important meeting of the Estates within his own life-time[2] (up to 1573). The development of this branch of the government offered the best opportunity to the Huguenots, for they were in a minority of about one to eight.[3] With no influence in Parlement, and no chance of obtaining any, except by a possible conversion here or there, without a voice in the king's council since the death of Coligny, they chose to support the only purely elective body, hoping thereby to achieve at least a field for debate, albeit against a majority.

Hotman's equipment as a publicist was good from a theoretical standpoint, but he had had absolutely no firsthand experience of governmental responsibility. What he knew best was the functioning of the Roman Republic and Empire, life in medieval France and Germany, as depicted by chroniclers with a superstitious philosophy of history and a tendency to hero worship. As a closet philosopher he was inclined to stress the claim of precedent over the claim of expediency, to declare that a thing was good because it was sanctioned and

[1] Hotman to Bullinger, 12 December, 1572, printed in the *Rev. Hist.*, II (1876), 57.

[2] See his letter to Bon. Amerbach of 6 January, 1558, Basel, G II 19, fol. 119; and to Peter Martyr, 22 January 1561, in *Rev. Hist.* II (1876), 28.

[3] Romier and Ehinger are agreed on this proportion before St. Bartholomew.

hallowed by use, because its roots were in the dim past, rather than because it worked well in the present.

It is true that he had read widely; we find evidence in letters and books of an acquaintance with Plato, Aristotle, Demosthenes, Cicero, many of the later Romans, Marsiglio, Machiavelli, and Claude de Seyssel. He had had close contact with men in great place, and had thus indirectly come in touch with their problems, such as the codification of law desired by de l'Hôpital. The presence of many Englishmen in Strassburg during the 'fifties, while his mind was still formative, may have turned his thoughts towards the advantages of constitutional government. To be sure, Tudor England did not offer the highest degree of self-expression to the people, but there was a tradition, a phraseology dating from the fourteenth century, and a suitable machinery of government, which in the past had stated the mind of the nation, and would do so again, when depreciation in money values and appreciation in divinity of kingship should have made the occasion ripe.

It is possible that republican Switzerland may have offered something to his thought.[1] It would be difficult to generalise on the Swiss government during this period. It was still in the stage of free cities, with a rather loose union to offer a combined front against the Habsburgs. Hotman's experience had been of two cities, Lausanne and Geneva. The former had had its Plaid General from the fourteenth century until the Bernese conquest in 1536. Geneva had passed from the hands of a bishop into the power of an oligarchy, and finally had invited Calvin to put her house in order. This experiment in government probably had made a deep impression upon the young Hotman. Its attempt at moral reform

[1] Papire Masson, a follower of the Queen Mother, accuses him of doctrines "tabernae Helvetiorum popinae vino madentes". Quoted in Labitte, *Les prédicateurs de la Ligue* (Paris, 1841), p. lv.

would have served to dignify the function of the State, to place it side by side with the Church as a great force for spiritual uplift. That Geneva had formed this State on a basis of popular consent, and feigned to maintain it with popular co-operation seemed to bring it very near perfection. At the time of his second visit, Calvin had passed on, but Geneva had continued in the way her great leader had shown, although inclining more and more towards aristocracy.

An adaptation of this politico-religious State was the bond of union between the various Huguenot parishes in France. There was self-expression, probably restrained and guided by the pastor, who in turn had been instructed by Calvin. It must have been in a community of this type that Hotman had worshipped in Bourges. The Calvinist organisation had as its unit the separate congregation, which served also as a basis for taxation and as a military cadre. Twice a year or oftener neighboring congregations met together in a colloquy. Over this was the provincial synod, that might legislate for the individual colloquies of which it was composed, although the final authority was the national synod. The official organisation of the Huguenot church had taken its beginning at Orleans, where sweeping municipal privileges had given rise to marked republican tendencies. This was in 1557; in three years there were over two thousand reformed churches in France. After the peace of Amboise (1563) which permitted Calvinists to worship outside of Paris, the nation was divided into nine ecclesiastical provinces, linked together in a close confederation after 1565. In so far as church members were concerned, this was a democratic system of government, thrifty and efficient, which must have brought into sharp relief the autocratic and shiftless ways of the monarchy.

In addition to the experience of other thinkers and of other lands, over and above the model supplied by ecclesiastical organisations, was the incentive supplied by Hotman's own private misfortunes. Due to his change of religion, he had been deprived of an inheritance justly his; due to his unswerving loyalty to that faith, he was not able to obtain restitution through the proper legal channels, nor did the government offer any protection to life, limb or property; on several occasions royal agents had even taken a hand in the pillage. When he recalled that his lot was but the common lot of probably 2,000,000 Frenchmen, who paid tribute to an administration that did extremely little in return, he naturally sought a theory of government which might afford a voice to that much abused minority. Petition and appeal had failed to win grace; treaties were dishonored; the only remaining argument was deposition as unfit for office.

In a *Quaestio* published in 1573, presumably earlier than *Franco-Gallia,* he outlined rapidly the theories which are expanded in the longer book. His problem is the disposition of French territory, but in the discussion he managed to develop his idea of kingship as a trust, to be held only during good behaviour.

"It is an ancient and well-known problem" he says "whether rulers have the right voluntarily to diminish the realm and outlying possessions (regna et ditiones). It is famous not only in France, where the powers of the king are constantly in dispute (ubi de dominio Regis disputari solet) but also in Germany."

Whatever contribution Roman law makes to this question, is apparently on the side of the ruler. He quotes authors and historical evidence of this interpretation of the imperial jurisprudence. But in his opinion the matter demands somewhat more subtle treatment than it has hitherto received.

A fourfold division is made of those things which are under the rule and in the power of Caesar. Some are called res Caesaris, others res fisci, others public, others private. The things of Caesar are those which are in the private patrimony of each prince, as he is Honorius or Ludovicus. Those things are called fiscal which are not so much in the patrimony of the prince, as in that of the princeship, for the maintenance of its dignity,—somewhat like a civil list, to be applied to current expenses. Public goods are those which belong to the people and the State such as the treasure, and the common land of the body politic (? *civitatum*). This would imply that some part of the revenue would be diverted from the fisc to the people and the cities, i.e. not all of it is for royal use. The last group comprises those private possessions which are said to be in the patrimony of each citizen. According to the usually accepted view of Roman law, all four of these lay in the grant of Caesar. But Hotman thinks that this is an erroneous generalisation of very special circumstances. He quotes in refutation not a distinct statute, but a general principle, "ubi procuratori Caesaris non aliendae, sed bene gerendae rei potestas permissa esse traditur", and explains that possessions may belong to the king in a universal sense, but as units they are private property. He concludes that kings have not the right to alienate their territories without the advice and consent of their subjects, for it is not only the fields and houses, but also the inhabitants which are handed over. According to the principle just quoted, these people are not so much in his *power,* as in his *patronage;* not submitted to his power, but committed to his faith and benevolence. Subjects are not sought for the sake of kings, but kings for the sake of subjects; there can exist subjects without kings, but not kings without subjects.

Rule may be obtained through one of four different causes: (1) Either the kingdom is offered with the approval of the people, as in the case of the Polish election of 1573 or (2) it is given in succession from the preceding generation or (3) it is willed by a foreigner or (4) conquered in warfare. In the first case, it is obvious that any prerequisite pacts must be fulfilled, for the king who violates the public faith, ought not to be considered a king, but outside (expers) human faith and international law. If there was no pact, but simply a transference of rule, then also, since a king is a guide, not a destroyer of the State, he must observe the rule for curators, not to alter the law of the State. The author stresses again, that administration alone is granted to administrators, not the power of alienation. The king should play the role of guardian to his people. In the case of conquest, it may seem fitting that the prince should govern according to his own will. But after all, he did not achieve the victory singlehanded, but through the efforts of his own followers, so he cannot act without their common consent and advice.

Having eliminated by an appeal to logic every possible pretext for arbitrary rule founded on possession of the kingship, having repudiated also the claim of tradition founded on Roman law, he proceeds to a thesis which he does not uphold adequately until the publication of *Franco-Gallia,* i.e. in France our king can alienate or mortgage nothing without the consent of the public council of the people (commonly called the States General) as all the lawyers and even Baldus himself testifies.

CHAPTER III

HOTMAN: FRANCO-GALLIA

FROM Sedan, in October, 1573, Jacopus Castellus wrote to Hotman,

> Of a sudden came to us an uncertain rumor of your Franco-Gallia. Soon after a single copy from the Frankfort fair was brought here. Although I have not had chance to read it, I have skimmed through the dedication [and]. . . . immediately recognised—not the lion. . . . from his talons,—but the father from the form of the offspring. . . . I rejoice to perceive that you have not been broken in spirit. . . . but have sought aid and consolation in adversity from those same studies which were the delight of happier days.[1]

The book was dedicated to the Elector Palatine, a Protestant prince whose aid for the Huguenots was needed. In the midst of compliments to a sovereign who had ruled a contented people for sixteen years, the author explains his purpose in writing *Franco-Gallia.*

> Oppressed by realisation of the calamities and common miseries, I took to turning the pages of all the French and German historians, who have written of the polity of France. . . . [Our ancestors] maintained a sure footing in public affairs for the space of a thousand years. . . . proving that they were wise men. . . . So I became convinced that the only true remedy for all our evils was to return to the ways of our forefathers.[2] . . . . Now the misfortunes that have befallen our Common-

[1] *Epistolae . . . Hotomannorum* (Amsterdam, 1700), p. 39.

[2] Hotman, *Franco Gallia* (Cologne, 1574), Preface, sine pag.

wealth are. . . . attributed to our civil dissensions, [but] I found upon inquiry that these are not so properly to be called the Cause as the Beginning of our mischiefs. . . . I affirm the cause to have been the great Blow which our Constitution received about one hundred years ago from the Prince who first of all broke in upon the noble and solid institutions of our ancestors.[1]

He reverts to the Platonic comparison of the natural body and the body politic and asserts that as true health cannot be attained after dislocation until every member be in its proper place, so the commonwealth cannot function until it be restored to its natural state. To this end he purposes to give an account of the laws and ordinances of France as far as may tend to the service of the commonwealth. Since his argument is precedent as the sole excuse for being, he is compelled to return to the earliest known (or hazily known) history of his native land, the days of pre-Roman Gaul. The authorities for this period are Caesar, Strabo, and Tacitus. The country was disunited; there were monarchies and aristocracies, but each one had a common council, meeting annually, to discuss the interests of the state. There were yearly elections of magistrates, but in the monarchies the king held his office for life. He had not unlimited authority, however, for he was bound by the law, even as the people were.[2]

Gaul under the Romans was restive. Its conquered people yearned for their former free institutions and appealed to the Franks for assistance. Hotman rejects the fable which connects the Franks with the Trojans. He says rather tartly that the history of Guillaume du Bellay, upholding this thesis, is a romance like Amadis of Gaul. In his opinion, the

[1] *Franco-Gallia* (London, 1711), Preface, p. v.

[2] Quoting Caesar, *De Bello Gallico*, Book V, Chapter 8.

Franks were Germans, who lived in the marshy lands along the Scheldt, neighbors of the Batavians. After an indecisive battle against the Romans, other German tribes offered an alliance to the combined Franco-Gallic forces. This event gives the author an opportunity to apostrophise the contemporary Germans and French.

May the omen prove lucky! and may the Francs truly and properly deserve that name, who after having shaken off that yoke of slavery imposed upon them by tyrants, have thought fit to preserve to themselves a commendable liberty, even under the domination of kings. For to obey a king is not servitude. Neither are all who are governed by kings. . . . for that reason to be counted slaves, but such as submit themselves to the unbounded will of a tyrant, a thief, and executioner, as Sheep resign themselves to the knife of the Butcher. The Francs had always Kings. . . . and when they constituted Kings, they never intended they should be Tyrants. . . . but keepers of their liberties,—protectors, Governors, and tutors.[1]

The next topic is the matter of selecting a king. Having previously shown that the Franks were German, Hotman justifiably attributes to them the accepted elective method of other German tribes, and notes that even at the time of writing Poles, Germans, Danes, and Swedes still have an elective monarchy, in which the sons of former kings, although they are preferred candidates, do not necessarily inherit the throne. " Those that constitute a commonwealth are much mistaken if they have more regard to kindred than to the qualification of the Prince they are about to set over them." After quoting from various chronicles to show that the right of election actually was exercised, he goes on to the complementary function of deposition, " that it may be understood, how great was the right and authority of the Estates (ordinum) and the people in making and supporting their kings ". At the end

[1] *Franco-Gallia* (London, 1711), p. 30.

of a list of examples of forced abdication,—occasionally of tyrannicide—he comments

This most glorious and famous deed of our ancestors deserves the more diligently to be remarked, for having been done at the very beginning and infancy of that kingdom; as if it had been a denunciation and declaration, that the Kings of Franco-Gallia were made such upon definite known terms and conditions; and were not tyrants with absolute unlimited and arbitrary power.

There was no well established precedent in the selection of candidates.[1] Sometimes the kingdom was divided among two or three kings; in other cases it seemed better to unite under one leader. The judgment of the Estates was the decisive factor.

Once elected king, how great was the authority of the monarch? We have seen that his will was subordinate to the laws; in addition he had not complete ownership of land and other capital goods. This takes Hotman into a discussion on the classification of national wealth which he had already covered in the Quaestio. If the crown should be transferred, according to elective privileges, from one house to another, and if it should be fitting to support in dignity the children of the deceased king, an appropriation must be made from class one—the royal domain—with the approval of the estates.[2] Nothing else may be touched, for the next two groups are necessary for the upkeep of the government, the fourth is the private property of the individual citizen. Unless Hotman meant that the king had some possessions under class four, this argument, carried to its logical conclusion, would imply that the king had no private property at all, since even that which is his " as Ludovicus or Honorius ", must be

[1] No one under twenty-four might be elected. Charles IX was twenty-three in 1573.

[2] *Franco-Gallia* (Cologne, 1574), Chapter 7.

granted to his children by the Estates. In the edition of 1586, Chapter IX, Hotman corrects this situation.

To the Frankish kings had been granted not only fiscal rights . . . but also certain definite farms to be used for the maintenance of the royal dignity, which in the vernacular are called the royal domain. . . . This domain is somewhat like the dowry of the kingdom. . . . or . . . . like the usufruct of certain possessions, because the complete ownership (proprietas) of these possessions remains lodged with the people, nor can any part be alienated by the king, without popular authority, that is, without the consent of the Estates. . . . It should be clear from this definition, how great is the difference between the royal patrimony and the royal domain. For the patrimony is the peculiar property of the king himself, but the domain is the property of the kingdom (regni) or as is vulgarly said, of the Crown (Coronae). The former is rightfully the king's, and he has the fullest authority to alienate it if he wishes. But of the latter, the proprietorship rests with the people as a whole (universitatem populi)."

He makes a distinction between the uses to which the revenues from the domain and the fiscal revenue may be put. The land has been appropriated for the living expenses of the king himself, whereas the money was granted for the upkeep of the State. If on account of war or other necessities, the amount seems insufficient, then a further grant in aid can be made with the assent of the Estates. It is interesting to observe that Hotman sanctions commercial operations with regard to the fisc, although he bars them in reference to the domain.

Chapter Eight constitutes a digression which bestrays the polemical nature of the whole book. It makes an attempt to disprove the Salic Law as part of the French law of succession. The Salic Law, according to Hotman, was a law of inheritance for real property among the Salian Franks. It was thus not public but private law which forbade the transference of allodial land to women, through inheritance. In an emergency when the throne was claimed by Edward III of England, the son of a French princess, the Salic Law was assumed to be a royal law, which prevented his legitimate accession.

Having demolished the legal obstacle to the rule of women, Hotman proceeds to describe another and more terrifying barrier, the abuses of female rule. Even so sage a guardian as Blanche of Castile is depicted as a jealous tyrant. Of course his object is to suggest the rule of Catherine; he seems to ignore the possibility of giving offense to Elizabeth, on whose aid the Huguenots were relying; to ignore also the irrelevance, in a disquisition on the elective character of the French monarchy, of a harangue on the unfitness of women to reign, or to act as regent. Presumably the wisdom of the councillors would eliminate any female candidates without second thought. In fact this chapter rather weakens than strengthens the chain of argument.

The form and constitution of the Franco-Gallican government which has been delineated in various foregoing passages is resumed and expanded in two chapters on the contractual nature of the State, and the authority of the general assembly. The kingdom set up by the fusion of Gallo-Romans and German Franks took over the constitution of their commonwealth from the conquering Germans, and was a tempered or mixed state, with components of every type—a king, an aristocracy, and deputies from each province to represent democracy. The executive was elected to office for life, on condition that he respect the laws, with certain reservations of authority to the nation. Supreme administration was lodged in the public council, which met on the Kalends of May, to discuss the great affairs of the Republic, and to take decisions with the common consent and advice of all the Estates. The wisdom of this institution appears in the following advantages: (1) in the multitude of prudent counsellors the weight and excellence of counsel shows itself more apparently; (2) it is an essential part of liberty that the same persons at whose cost and peril a thing is done, should have it done likewise by their authority and advice; (3) ministers of State having influence with the prince, may be kept in control by this council, in which the grievances of the subject are freely laid open.

Too great a risk is incurred in handing over the fate of a nation to the judgment of a single person, who lacks the many-sided vision of a group, acting by united counsels and guided by one spirit, composed and made up of the minds of many wise men. Referring to the public assemblies of Greece, of the Holy Roman Empire, of England, and of Aragon, Hotman reaches the conclusion

'Tis very plain that this most valuable liberty of holding a common council of the Nation, is not only a party of the people's right, but that all kings, who by Evil Arts do oppress or take way this Sacred Right ought to be esteemed violators of the Laws of Nations and, being no better than Enemies of Human Society, must be considered not as Kings but as Tyrants.

The detailed powers of this assembly are government-making, in so far as it may create and depose the monarch, (2) legislative, dealing only with public law, but probably without initiative, (3) administrative, in handling affairs of State and of religion, in conferring public honors, in assigning a patrimony to the king's children, and (4) sharing with the king certain executive powers such as declaring war, and appointing magistrates to office. One wonders if so vast a program could have been carried out in one session in the Springtime.

There is an explanation of the essential differences between the rex and the regnum. The king is the head of the

State, but the kingdom is the collectivity of citizens, and as it were, the body of the State. Hence the office of the king is to care for the well-being and happiness of his subjects. Furthermore, the king is mortal, but the kingdom lasts forever. The king may lose his mind, he is a prey to constant temptation, but the kingdom has in its elders and nobles (Senioribus et Optimatibus), skilled in practical affairs, a sure and definite sagacity of its own. He clearly sees the king as a temporary embodiment of kingship, which in its turn is a mere agency for the execution of the will of the nation, limiting nation rather narrowly to the upper classes of the population.

The fourth edition goes into a detailed discussion as to the precise limits wherein the royal power acts but as it includes some deviations from Hotman's original theory of election, it has been postponed for later treatment.

Certain attacks were made upon the constitution by the third race of kings, the Capetians, in that they gradually took over from the council the power of ministerial appointment. Their own nominees held office for life, which was contrary to precedent, and frequently handed it on to their sons. This built up a strong and independent aristocracy, to the detriment of the central government. The Estates however continued to play their part during governmental crises, intervening in the peace negotiations after Poitiers, nullifying the will of Charles V, and taking control during the insanity of Charles VI. The most crushing blow to the assembly was dealt by Louis XI, at the time of the War of the Public Weal. An attempt had been made to impose upon the king an advisory council of thirty-six, drawn from all three estates. He yielded until the rebellion had been quelled, then violated his promise, and defied the assembly. From that time the government had been out of joint. The civil dissensions were but symptons of a more fundamental ailment—the lack of constitutional safeguards.

As the Estates grew less important, the law courts took over some of their prerogatives. No magistrate could take office until he had given his oath to the Parlement. No royal edict was in force until it had been registered by the maîtres. Any appeal must be lodged with the Grand' Chambre.

The book ends abruptly and inconsequentially with a diatribe against the self-seeking cupidity of the lawyers.

Some of the inspiration for this work must have been found in the views of Michel de l'Hôpital. In the address which he delivered to the Estates of Orleans, December, 1560, he elaborated upon their former importance. "It is certain that ancient kings used frequently to summon the Estates, made up of deputies from all their subjects." But de l'Hôpital considered their functions advisory and informative rather than administrative or executive. "The king discusses . . . the most weighty affairs, takes their advice, hears also their grievances. . . . Kings originally were elected for the purpose of rendering justice."[1] When plaints became too numerous for his individual attention, Parlement was founded to take care of private cases, but the pleas of the nation were still heard in the Estates. However, "it was contrary to custom to accept any edict before it had been accepted by the Parlement of Paris, the only depository of the Estates General, which it represented."[2]

Molinaeus, an early friend, had written a treatise on the antiquity of the kingdom, and its ancient laws, which he made a vehicle for a veiled attack on the idolatry of Catholicism. Hotman took over this machinery to attack not religion directly, but the existing government, in the cause of religion.

The book of Seyssel, which he quotes here and there, par-

[1] *Recueil de pièces . . . concernant la tenue des États Généraux* (Paris, 1789), vol. i, p. 45.

[2] De l'Hôpital, *Oeuvres* (Paris, 1824), vol. ii, p. 79.

ticularly in the later edition, was a panegyric of the reign of Louis XII, but Seyssel managed to convey also an ardent admiration for a constitutional monarchy, for which France had an adequate machinery were it but properly set in motion. Hotman aimed at a similar goal, with minor differences in 1573 which he abandoned in 1586.

Since he based his argument on precedent, the historicity of the alleged facts becomes a significant step in the proof. He has been sniffed at for propounding an absurdity. France was certainly not a constitutional monarchy in the sixteenth century. To reason from this obvious situation back to a past which had strong constitutional leanings was disloyalty to the reigning monarch, and a confession of weakness. But if it is difficult to prove that the early Frankish kingdom was an elective monarchy, restrained at least by custom, it would be equally difficult to prove that it was *not* so. Our information is slight in any case, and hardly technical. What we know of Germanic tribes of a somewhat earlier date would indicate a fair degree of political liberty. Hotman assumes that this continued; he could only assume, because there were no contemporary writers of an education and intelligence capable of forming an estimate and conveying the type of information to which a Roman had readily turned. The chronicles which he had read, and faithfully reported, mention incidents which bear out his theory. They mention other incidents which give a contrary interpretation. The resultant would indicate that there was no fixed custom in a period of flux. The Church of Rome, the only institution which had preserved any momentum through the wreck of established things, had sprung from democratic beginnings. According to Tacitus, the Germans also had had a democratic rule. With these two traditions behind him, the balance seems to sway ever so slightly in Hotman's favor.

Of course the work is propaganda; the goal was set before

the evidence was selected. It is amusing to see how carefully the author himself evaluates the documents. In discussing the disappearance of the Merovingian line, even though authorities uphold the merits of the new house, yet, says he

> in reading such authorities, we ought to take this observation along, that since Pipin and his sons labored . . . . under a great load of envy . . . . they made it their business to find out and employ plausible ingenious historians who magnified the cowardice of Childeric and his predecessors, upbraiding them with sloth and idleness beyond what they deserved.[1]

He prefers to believe that Pipin was elected by the assembly rather than appointed by the pope, though "there is scarce an author who does not acquiesce in the testimony of one Pope concerning the power of another".[2]

As France progressed from anarchy to feudalism and thence to centralisation, the value of the historical argument in favor of the council declined. The feudal court grew into the royal curia, struggled to hold its place, but only in isolated instances, when there was no competition from the crown, was it able to make itself felt. Certainly the kingship was not elective after the tenth century.

For a man of the mental grasp of Hotman, the work is singularly incoherent. The separate chapters are perfectly intelligible, but the book as a whole seems to lack articulation. There are too many digressions, such as an entire chapter devoted to the flowing hair of the Merovingians, and not sufficient emphasis on many important points. For instance, who had the right to sit in the Estates General? Was the suffrage universal? Just what were the customary constitutional checks, since there were no written laws? Did the king have any property of his own, which he might manage

[1] *Franco-Gallia* (London, 1738), p. 88.

[2] *Ibid.*, p. 91.

as he pleased? In other words, had he the rights of any ordinary citizen, or was he a mere puppet of the administrative body? The lack of stress, and the disproportionate space given to minor matters (possibly for the display of erudition) produce a blurred impression which is inconsistent with the ability of a journalist who could compose *Le Tigre.*

Hotman wrote to Capellus:

> Then too the book is historical; it is the history of a fact. The whole discourse is dependent upon fact. These people deny the truth of it. But what impudence, when hardly three statements are brought forward without testimony, and the clearest documents? If they complain that I have made an illogical statement, or invented a fact, or that I have swerved from truth to falsehood, let them bring this forward in print. I will undertake the debate at the peril of my head.[1]

Apparently he had convinced himself, even if the wish was father to the thought. The ideal government which he had created for the needs of the French Protestants, and of whose historic existence he was now firmly assured, was a monarchy limited by election, referendum and deposition. The idea of election was engendered by the necessity of eliminating the Catholic House of Valois, which still had two eligible males to succeed Charles IX. If we overlook the particular application, it is evident that the general theory would create a king in a position of dependence, which would only be increased by the further necessity of constant reference to the source of power. The extreme measure of a forced abdication leads on to the doctrine of tyrannicide, so characteristic of the later Calvinist school, but not prominent at this time. Calvin himself had counselled passive obedience in individual citizens.

[1] From Geneva, 2 March s. a. (1575?) printed in the *Epistolae*, p. 149.

Hotman's idealised king, then, is an agent of the sovereign power, the Estates General, of which one group at least was delegated from the third estate. He sometimes confuses the issue by the use of the word protector, or guardian, which might almost imply a benevolent despot, but the exposition of the work of the assembly vitiates this interpretation. The king's attitude towards the people should be paternal, but not in the sense that he is all wise and all powerful.

The assembly would seem similar in composition to the Tudor Parliament, in its selection of the upper layers of the bourgeoisie, but it is rather strange that the author avoids all mention of the first estate. He says repeatedly that the council should be made up of king, nobles and delegates from the people. Perhaps he meant to include the princes of the church among the nobility, or it may have been a problem which he had not yet solved. Reasoning historically, he would have had to admit them; reasoning pragmatically, he would have been loathe to allow the solidly hostile vote of one house. He is not any more explicit with regard to the third estate; we constantly come upon the expression, " delegates of the people ", which may be a reflexion of the democratic teachings that during this same century invited the country-folk to participate in the nomination of deputies. At the same time he quotes Polydore Vergil on the English Parliament: " For fear this Council should be cumbered with the opinions of an unskillful multitude (whose custom it is to distinguish nothing justly) it was at first established by a certain law what sort of Persons . . . should be called to this Council."

Whatever its composition,—and he would need to be careful about that, if he were to accomplish his immediate ends—there is no doubt that he recognised this body as the real ruler of the state. The powers which it delegated to king or magistrate reverted in time to the assembly. Whether the nation had handed over its sovereignty to this body, or whether the representatives had only mandatory powers, is not clear at this time. Perhaps the question of the ultimate source of legal sanction had not occurred to him. Indeed, he discussed two apparently opposing concepts,—fundamental laws which rested on the sanction of tradition, and an all powerful assembly which had full power to legislate in the field of public law.

As one critic has commented, Hotman somewhat paradoxically urged a democratic goal by appealing to historical precedent.[1] At the same time that he traced the development of the French Estates General, he did not neglect at least a passing use of the comparative method, in making reference to similar assemblies in other lands.

The dedication is dated 21st August, 1573. Capellus on the 31st October, reported the appearance of the first copy in Sedan. Its fame spread until the author planned to issue another edition,[2] " for the book (all who come hither from France affirm it) has great weight in explaining the right of the people against a tyrant ".[3] And later " The book is in the hands of all great men (magnatum). You would hardly believe, what anger it stirs up among our tyrants ".[4] In fact it was so popular that a pirated edition appeared in February, 1574. "I had forgotten [to mention] that our Franco-Gallia has been secretly translated and printed. . . . For the people of Berne requested, through the ambassador of Solothurn, that it should be . . . (sic) translated. In the meanwhile some friend of theirs surreptitiously . . . (sic) did

[1] Labitte, *op. cit.*, p. lv.

[2] H. to du Tilloy, 23 July, 1575, s. l. Bibl. Nat., Fonds Latin 8586 sine pag.

[3] H. to Basil Amerbach, Geneva, 12 July, s. a., Basel G II 19, fol. 167.

[4] To the same, Geneva, 5 October s. a., Basel G II 19, fol. 166.

this. I hope that they will be punished."[1] At the beginning of the following year

at Chambéry, three heralds in the public square of the Duke of Savoy and his Senate, forbade anyone to dare to sell, read, touch, or even to have this little book at home. When the news was received the typographers vied with each other in hurrying out a new edition.[2]

Capellus replied: "You know how hateful your name is just on account of this *Franco-Gallia,* which I see has stirred up such a commotion among the Savoyards. Why then you signed your name to it, I cannot understand: certainly many feel that this was ill-advised."[3] The French court was sufficiently disturbed to attempt a reply, through Masson, a retainer of Catherine de Medici. His attack Hotman contemptuously labelled "Italo-Gallia". Of another pamphlet by Matharellus, he says "I have seen the writing of Henry Matharellus, attacking our *Franco-Gallia,* [but it is] so crude, stupid, torpid, . . . that I can hardly decide how to answer him."[4] In three months the work had been completed. "Matharellus and Masson are answered as they deserve. In vain have the dogs been persuaded, by Semiramis, to bark."[5] The reply to the former is very dull. He chose as text Proverbs 26, "responde stulto secundum suam stultitiam". The *Strigilis Papirii Massoni* does explain one or two points which the first edition of *Franco-Gallia* had left obscure.

The fatuity of a scholar of Baudouin[6] appears on page six, where he says that it is a matter of grave doubt, whether the

[1] H. to Tossanus, Gra. (?), 1 March, 1574. Printed in *Epistolae,* p. 44.

[2] H. to Capellus, 7 January, 1575. Printed in the *Epistolae,* p. 46.

[3] Sedan, 13 February, 1575. *Epistolae,* p. 48.

[4] H. to Capellus, 20 April, s. a., *Epistolae,* p. 51.

[5] To same, 23 July s. a., *Epistolae,* p. 56.

[6] He had had a quarrel with Baudouin at Strassburg.

kings of France succeeded to the throne, or really were elected. But I . . . have said and shown that this question now-a-days is no more pertinent than whether the mother of Evander had more upper teeth, than lower: since it is certain that our kings for more than five hundred years have followed in succession. . . . Once upon a time, I say, and in very ancient times, kings were elected and deposed in the parlament of the three estates. . . . .[1]

For when this maniac, led on by bribery, wishes to belittle the prestige of the parlament of the three estates, that is, the custom of our ancestors, he says "the public council is Euripus [2] and the people are rarely guided by wisdom, but more often by wrath and impulse". Just as if the assembly of the three estates were directed by the plebs, and not (as Claude de Seyssel . . . shows in his Monarchia Franciae) by the delegates of the nobility and the cities [civitatum?] of France, who, since they excel all others in worth and wisdom and dignity, are elected, and sent with instructions and mandates to that parlament, that they may reveal to the royal majesty the necessities of the people and the exigencies of the commonwealth.

This definitely excludes the common people from the highest authority in the land. It would seem to imply, also, that the members of the assembly would look to their constituents as an authority more final than themselves, not in their voting capacity, but in their constitutional right to issue binding instructions. The classes sharing sovereignty, then, are the aristocracy and the burghers. Hotman still evades any mention of the clergy.

The course of events in France took a different turn after 1573 for in addition to the Huguenot party, and the strictly royal group, there was a third faction, the Politiques, comprising the more moderate members of the two foregoing,

[1] Hotman, *Strigilis Papirii Massoni* (Paris, 1577), pp. 19-20.

[2] The straits between Euboea and the main land?

[3] *Ibid.*, p. 26.

led by the younger brother of the king,[1] and defending principles very like those which Hotman had advocated. Their original agreement made at Milan in July, 1574, included religious liberty, and above all things, and by every means, a prompt convocation of the Estates.[2] In November of the same year their military leader, Damville, of the house of Montmorency, addressed the provincial estates of Languedoc, appealing to loyal subjects to help him secure a peaceable settlement of the religious dissensions. The means were the expulsion of foreigners, the convocation of the Estates, and the summoning of a general or national religious council.[3] In the Spring Hotman had written to Gualter at Zurich:

In Paris alone . . . more than a thousand persons, nobles, judges or merchants . . . have taken the name of politiques, and with the support of the brother of the king, they have asked that the old French constitution be revived, in calling the Estates General. It really is the only remedy for so many evils, but at the same time it is the heaviest blow which can be aimed at the tyrant's cause. The Queen Mother has got control, alleging I know not what promise of the king, [Charles IX had died in May] with as much impudence as ignorance, just as if the death of the mandatory did not put an end to the mandate, or as if one could will away something one did not own. Who can be unaware . . . no matter how little he knows our history, that the right of governing in interregna belongs to the Estates General and the Conseil? [4]

Two years later, there was still revolt in the South.

[1] F. Rocquain, *La France et Rome pendant les querres de religion* (Paris, 1924), p. 155.

[2] Rocquain, *op. cit.*, p. 181, quoting *Memoires de l'Estat de France . . .* t. III., pp. 292-296 and 301-305.

[3] F. C. Palm, *Politics and Religion in Sixteenth Century France* (Boston, 1927), p. 99, quoting Devic et Vaissette, *Histoire Générale de Languedoc*, vol. xii, pp. 1105-1111. Bibl. Nat., Coll. Brienne 207, fol. 136.

[4] Printed in the *Revue Historique*, II (1876), 374-375. Original at Zurich.

The Provencals, although enemies of the religion [reformed] nevertheless wearied by such everlasting tyranny, have commenced to demand their liberty. Last year the people of Marseilles came to blows with certain Italians. Indeed, what has never happened since the world has been world, since taxes have existed,—all the taxes, all the tolls of France are in the power of Italians. These people give the king a large sum of money, but one can hardly depict the harshness, the rigor and the cruelty they show in fleecing the poor Frenchmen.[1]

He was relieved to discover that the Huguenots did not stand alone. " It is fortunate for us that this demand for liberty has been started by others than by us. If the example succeeds, it will not lack imitators."[3]

In the same month (May, 1576) peace was signed—a peace supposedly achieved by the efforts of the Duke of Alençon, and hence known as the Peace of Monsieur. Its provisions read like a prophecy of the Edict of Nantes. There should be free exercise of the cult except in Paris. Temples could be constructed, synods, both national and provincial, might meet, Huguenots were to be admitted to the universities, to all offices and dignities, there were to be eight fortified places of surety, and in the parlements, chambers in which the judges were divided in equal numbers between the two faiths. Furthermore, the Estates were to assemble within six months.

Seemingly the Politiques had achieved what they set out to do, but a lit de justice was requisite before the Parlement of Paris would allow the treaty to become law. Cessation of hostilities did not effect any essential change in the position of Hotman. He declined to venture within French territory. The court made some feeble overtures to so vociferous an

[1] Hotman to Crato von Crafftheim, 19 May, 1576. Printed in the *Rev. Historique*, II (1876), 382. Original at Breslau.

[2] H. to Basil Amerbach, s. l., 9 May s. a. (1576?). Basel, G II 19, fol. 177.

adversary, and then decided to ignore him. "[The Queen Mother] has reconciled Alençon with his brother. . . . He has written me in his own hand . . . offering to attach me to him as maître des requêtes, with permission to live where I will. I am accepting this offer." [1] It would have been interesting to observe what change, if any, this appointment made in his theory of government, but a month later, Alençon had abandoned him. "He who had offered me so great an honor, with an emolument of 1200 livres . . . has yielded completely to his brother and mother, deserting us in our misfortune, if not betraying us." [2]

He continued his literary occupations, bringing out new editions of commentaries in use at the Universities. The Law School of Geneva had been opened by Donellus and Hotman in 1573. He had thus a slender revenue, supplemented by fees from private pupils. "Domina Cancellaria, the widow of the great de l'Hôpital, has sent her children to me, that I may read over the *Institutes* with them at home, and she has used so many wiles in besieging me, that plainly I am forced to put aside my other studies." [3] In a volume of consilia which appeared in May 1578 there is one that reverts to his contractural ideas, *De Conventionibus et Transactionibus inter Principem et Subditos*.[4] This is merely re-iteration of the point of view expressed in *Franco-Gallia:* "In these public conventions, an obligation is voluntarily contracted, that the aforesaid citizens are bound to their princes for the observation of these pacts, and in turn the princes and their successors are bound to the promise which they gave in these pacts, by all human and divine law." If the princes do not

[1] H. to Crato von Crafftheim, 29 November, 1576, *Rev. Historique*, II (1876), 384. Original at Breslau.

[2] H. to Bas. Amerbach, s. l., 8 January, 1577, Basel G II 19, fol. 183.

[3] To Bas. Amerbach, s. l., 22 January, 1578, Basel G II 19, fol. 195

[4] *Opera*, vol. II, Consilium 131.

keep their vows, their subjects are released from theirs, or they may even complain before imperial judges. However, the safest method is to protest, "ne dicam ei subjectionem, et obedientiam renunciare".

Hotman must have been engaged in some other work of a dangerous character at this time, for there is a hurried letter, addressed to N.N., dated March 18th, 1578,"

I have asked . . . our friend that he should tell you everything about the Landgrave's interdict, and about the prohibited edition of certain books. I implore you vehemently not to allow the little book to get about among the people, for I do not want to offend this prince, who has revealed to us the most important matters . . . of his council. Farewell . . . from my bed before dawn.

The success of *Franco-Gallia* had spread his fame abroad. Offers came from Strassburg, Leyden, and even far-off Brandenburg, but he refused these and chose instead to go to Basel, where he had friends, "who yesterday honored me and my arrival with a . . . banquet."[1] There is another letter, dated (I think incorrectly) 1583, explaining his reasons for leaving Geneva.

A few days before I left Geneva I received your most courteous letter. Since for three years we were living at Geneva in constant fear of war, which had caused us to leave our native land in the first place, conquered at length by the entreaties of my wife and children I betook myself to this haven,—if indeed there is any haven in this whole world for the miserable French. We have a French church here, established by the authority of the Senate, without which I cannot exist, nor should I permit my family to be deprived of it, as long as life shall be given to us. Of course, the skies are not so sunny as those of Geneva, to which we have grown accustomed during those six years [1572-

[1] To Gualter, at Zurich, 8 Sept., 1578, Bibl. Nat., Fonds Latin 8586.

1578]. . . . The home prepared for me by my friends is in a most charming spot, near to the Old Münster, in the house of the canons. You would hardly believe how changed is the appearance of my little daughters. I pray God that he may permit this tranquillity to be lasting.[1]

Although he appreciated the calm, he was not entirely satisfied with the religious situation.

I believe that this dissent from the pure Scripture is born from corruption and depravity of manners. What is there in common between the Evangel and such gluttony and drunkenness and extravagance as I had hoped never to see nor hear? Is it remarkable if God sends this frenzy of quarreling to such a group of men? I should prefer that discipline and improvement of morals be taken into consideration. We are a joke to the Romanists. Our doctrine is reformed, but our lives are deformed.[2]

Certain specific cases he felt demanded action.

That good printer Perna, who has been thrown into prison by the magistrates so many times on account of the impious and execrable books published by him, has printed here all the detestable works of Machiavelli, translated into Latin by that man Stupian. You know that his works on account of their open blasphemy against Moses and Christ may not be printed or sold at retail, even in Italy. Wolphus who died recently at Augsburg . . . calls Machiavelli the master of all crime, impiety, and sin, and states that in a certain place he has written that after death he would much prefer to go to the lower regions and the devils, than to ascend to heaven. For in heaven he would find no one but beggars and some wretched monks, hermits and apostles, but in the other place he would live with Cardinals, Popes, Kings, and Princes.[3] Yet this blasphemy was . . .

[1] H. to Stuckius, Basel, 8 September (1578?), Bibl. Nat., Fonds Latin 8586.

[2] H. to Gualter, Basel, 26 May, 1579, *Epistolae*, p. 111.

[3] This sentiment was not original with Machiavelli.

spread abroad with the privilege of the Lord Rector of Basel, translated into Latin by the very man who . . . for a long time was supported on the alms of the Senate, [but] is now the husband of a wealthy second wife. This man, when he was fulfilling the office of Rector two years ago, dared to say . . . to me, that he did not know that the Roman mass was blasphemy: nor did he concern himself with such things. When I heard this I hastened to Zulcer, Amerbach, and Zwinger, hoping that they would give me the opportunity of rebuking him before the College. I will not tell you the answer which I received. With downcast face I returned in silence to my home, marvelling at the religion of Basel, and almost stupefied at these recent events. The avenging of such profanity (not to call it anything worse) I have left to God." [1]

It seems a pity that there was no outlet for such perfervid energy. Condé wrote, asking in his own name, and in that of the King of Navarre, that Hotman would go to the assembly of princes at Nuremberg to plead their cause before the Emporor and defend their church. The heir to the duchy of Hesse also urged this move. But Hotman was loathe to go: " My age of fifty-five years keeps me from their suggestion of new journeys ". His friends were vexed. Gualter wrote from Zurich,

I cannot see why you refuse [to fulfill] your duty to the French Church. The journey is neither long nor dangerous. If Casimir [the son of the Grand-duke of Hesse] should go, you could join his group, and watch for an opportunity, if English ambassadors or our own should go, to attach yourself to them. In the meanwhile you could suggest wise plans to Casimir and the others. [2]

The meeting did not accomplish much. The Emperor Rudolph was more interested in obtaining levies for the defense

[1] H. to Gualter 25 December, 1580, s. l., *Epistolae*, p. 139.

[2] 12 August, 1580, *Epistolae*, p. 133.

of Austria than in spending money for the assistance of the Huguenots. " In his request the first place was given to that same old tune of the Austrians (vetus Austricorum cantilena)—collecting funds to drive off the Turks and to strengthen Hungarian fortifications." [1]

Jean Hotman, the eldest of his sons, had been sent to England to be educated in the household of Poulet, the English ambassador to France. There is a letter addressed to the "envoy of the most serene queen" that touches rather a pathetic strain:

Although I had been extremely sollicitous about my son Jean, yet I have had letters from him in which he tells me that he has been received into your family most kindly. . . . Certainly I judge my son most fortunate, and myself also, because by the remarkable kindness of God, it has happened that he came upon such a situation with such a man. For from the time when God gave me children, my first consideration has been to bring them up with a sense of duty and self-respect. Thirty long years have now passed since on account of zeal for piety I have either been away from my native land, parents and relatives, or else grievously harassed in my own country, bearing greater hardships than among foreigners who were strangers. And so, although I have never lived a slothful and idle life, but have always pursued a most energetic type of existence, and have carried out the work of teaching the young; nevertheless, tossed about by so many fierce waves and tempests, I cannot prepare any other inheritance for my children, than hope and faith in God's mercy. . . . If I should have the opportunity of rendering any service to you and yours, I promise that you shall find me neither ungrateful nor forgetful.[2]

A few years later Poulet gave Jean an opportunity to go to Oxford with his sons. The younger Hotman wrote to his father telling with some animation of his studies.

[1] Gualter to Hotman, 15 July, 1582, *Epistolae*, p. 156.

[2] Basel, 1 April, 1579. *Epistolae*, p. 107.

There is not much interest here in the civil law . . . in the meanwhile I have acquired a knowledge of Italian, German and English. . . . To these things I am drawn not by cool judgment, nor any necessity, but simply by natural propensity; I have even started Spanish recently. . . . English History pleases me, since it sheds great light on that of France.[1]

The plague swept through Eastern France and Switzerland in 1583. At the time that Jean was writing to his father, his mother was dying, and with her loss the old restlessness came upon Hotman. Basel was Lutheran; he left it for Geneva.

Believe me, there is no need for condolence, but rather for congratulation that I and my family have escaped from that Basilean solitude hither into the companionship of so many friends, relatives, and associates. A wretched and woe-begone life have I led on account of the absence of friends whose agreeable and sympathetic company I here enjoy, with my children.[2]

He was hardly re-established in Geneva before an opportunity arrived to write for his cause. Letters came from Henry of Navarre, heir presumptive since the death of Alençon, and Duplessis-Mornay, asking the aid of Hotman's pen in replying to attacks by the Guise party. " A book has been written and published against him [Henry] at the instance of the House of Guise, by which he is declared incapable of succeeding to the crown.[3] The king of Navarre wrote:

[1] Oxford, 20 April, 1583. Bibl. Nat., Fonds Latin 8586. In the same collection is a complimentary letter from Jean Hotman to Sir Philip Sidney, s. l. s. a.

[2] H. to Stuckius, 6 November, 1584. *Epistolae*, pp. 181-182.

[3] Duplessis-Mornay to Hotman, St. Germain, 3 December, 1584. Printed in *Archives du Musée Teyler*, Série II, vol. xii, Deuxième Partie (Haarlem, 1911), P. J. Blok, Editor, " Correspondance inédite de . . . Fr. Hotman," p. 204.

" Your writings have been so happily received in all Christendom, the memory is so praiseworthy and your desire for the public welfare is so well known to all, that I . . . implore you to deal with this matter . . . Vostre meylleur et byen assuré amy, Henry ".[1] De Buzanval, Henry's ambassador to London, reveals that the Catholic party are using Hotman's own book as an argument against the Huguenot leader.

Your doctrine and reputation have given such influence to your writings that passages taken from them serve as so many irreproachable witnesses when they are used against you, as so many condemnations without appeal. That is the reason why several people, eager to abuse your name, have turned to their own advantage certain passages of your *Franco-Gallia* for the election of the kings of France.[2]

Further instructions followed in the Spring from Henry's chancellor, Arnaud du Ferrier:

I wrote to tell you of the great satisfaction with which I have seen and read what you sent to M. Duplessis. This agrees with the opinion which I have always held, that the succession . . . has nothing in common with feuds and still less with other hereditary and divisible things, but that they ought to go from the eldest to the next, and to the chief nearest representative of the stock. . . . Unless I am mistaken, it has been done thus in the past. You are the only one of contrary judgment. My opinion would be that the result ought not to be taken into consideration, but simply the prerogative . . . of him who is the chief descendant of the said stock.[3]

Two nearly contemporary letters of Duplessis-Mornay give him the bases on which to build—" You ought to deduce our right from the constitutional law (*jure et lege*) of the king-

[1] From Montauban, 24 August, 1584, Blok, p. 204.

[2] 30 December, 1584, Blok, p. 209.

[3] 7 May, 1585, Blok, p. 214.

dom rather than from natural equity (*justa re*) in this particular case, and to argue from feudal law rather than ancient law". In July he repeated the advice, "You must deduce our right from the law of the kingdom, or rather from feudal and French law, than a *justa re*".

The treatise *De Jure Successionis* was completed in 1585. It contains a considerable amount of repetition of the sentiments of *Franco-Gallia,* but of course the idea of an elective monarchy had to be dropped. As he says in the preface, he took up the work with the hope of doing a service to his afflicted country—"perhaps the last service to be rendered by an old man, nearly decrepit"—, and set himself the task of putting into writing customs which through the approval of many centuries, had taken on force of written law. He quotes as authorities a long list of royal councillors and judges of Parlement.

The seven chapters, which like those of *Franco-Gallia,* have little order of development, might be grouped under three heads: those dealing with the succession (I, IV, II, III); one dealing with a regency (V); two discussing chiefly alienation of territory, but covering in addition royal finances, and the characteristics of the State.

He re-affirms, as he had once declared in *Franco-Gallia,* that the kingdom cannot be willed away by the king. It rests with the nation to grant the kingship, but instead of using the elective process, the nation recognises the claims of tradition, of unwritten custom, sanctified by the use of six hundred years, and calls upon the eldest son of the defunct, or the grandson, if his father has predeceased him. In exceptional cases, where there is no direct male heir, the nearest branch of the royal house shall ascend the throne, in the person of the male heir, standing in direct descent through eldest sons. Hotman goes into this very carefully. To have said "the eldest male agnate" would have opened a way for the claims of Cardinal Charles de Bourbon, a younger brother of Antony of Navarre, hence the uncle of Henry. His religion made him an unwelcome candidate to the Huguenots. There are some rather unusual claims made for the king-elect, such as the title, an appanage, and a share in the power, which were intended to strengthen the position of Henry of Navarre as successor to Henry III.[1]

No women, bastards, or legitimated sons may ascend the throne.

In the case of a minority, the name of king shall be given to the boy, but the power shall remain with the princes and procurators of the kingdom, as constituted in the public council. He quotes in support of this view, John Terrarubeus, Philip de Commines, and the wills of Charles V and of Louis XI.

The sixth law which states that land cannot be alienated by the king without the consent of the public counsel, goes again into the fourfold classification given in the *Quaestio,* and in *Franco-Gallia,* to stress the fact that the ruler holds the land in trust for the kingdom. Hotman compares the king to a vassal, the nation to the feudal lord. The king cannot hand on the kingdom to his son, but yields it, at death, to his lord, who then confirms it to the successor, with appropriate ceremonies.

The domain and the fisc do not differ essentially.

For this reason the Cour des Aides meets at Paris, so that there cases pertaining to the royal domain may be argued. Once upon a time the king's treasure consisted of nothing but the proceeds and return of the domain of the Crown of France; there were no tributes, indictions or taxes.

Tribute was granted on special occasions, for impending war, and was no greater than the immediate cause demanded.

[1] *Opera,* Lyons, 1599, vol. iii, book ii.

In those days " kings could not alter money; that is, increase or decrease the value of the coin " (appealing for confirmation to Budé and Molinaeus).

There are three possible interpretations of the word regnum; it may mean that region in which royal rule is set up; or it may mean the government, or administration of the king (regimen); or, finally the State,

> which is a very different thing from the rule of the king. No one would ask an explanation of the first two, but in the name of the State are included both *civitas* and people, who have given themselves over to the king, as to a guardian, to be protected and governed by definite laws; here it may be understood that the people retain for themselves the right of protecting their safety and their country against the desires of the king.

In resuming the whole, he says

> We can understand from the foregoing that the rights of the kings of the French are so constituted that they have not unlimited power of misusing the kingdom and their own rule, they may not dissipate the patrimony of the kingdom by immoderate gifts . . . . but that they must preserve intact the prosperity of their native land and people which was committed to their charge . . . . finally they must observe that most sacred precept of Tully, " That the guardianship or procuration of the State ought to be executed for the advantage of those who are controlled, not to the advantage of those who are in control.

This essay is not inconsistent with the fundamental thesis of *Franco-Gallia.* The author has made special concessions to the interests of the Navarrese candidates, by recognising that not election but custom establishes the right of succession to the crown. However if we recall that in the pamphlet *Strigilis Papirii Massonis,* he sarcastically comments that the kings of France have not been elected for over five hundred years, we can hardly accuse him of a shift of front. In other respects he clings to his ideal of a monarchy tempered by aristocracy. As the work is so brief, he has no space to mention the burghers, to whom he had granted some political power in the earlier book.

The question of the succession was causing serious difficulties. Henry was of course the legitimate heir, but many patriotic Frenchmen were troubled at the thought of a king who was not of the ancient faith, who could not be the eldest son of the Church. Catherine de Medici was anxious to obtain the crown for her daughter, Claude, wife of the Duke of Lorraine; Philip II hoped that his daughter Isabella, whose mother also had been a daughter of Catherine, might ascend the throne. The hesitation of the Roman Catholic loyalists was still further increased by the bull of excommunication launched against Henry in 1586.[1] Again the Navarrese party had recourse to Hotman:

> I think that you have seen the excommunication which the Pope has hurled against the King of Navarre and M. le Prince de Condé, to which some response must be made, and since the same lord king knows no one in all Christendom who can do this better than you, he has asked me to appeal to you.[2]

The following year appeared the *Brutum Fulmen Papae Sixti V* . . . containing the usual diatribes against the papacy, poured forth with the author's accustomed vehemence. Hotman had word that, if rumors were true, the Catholic party deigned to take notice.

[1] Ac plane tertia regni pars clamabat millies mori malle, quam Navarrum Regem ferre: a Papa excommunicatum et incapacem hereditatis regni pronuntiatum. Hotman to Grynaeus, Geneva, 20 December, 1586, Basel, G II 6, fol. 449.

[2] Jacques de Ségur to Hotman, 2 November, 1585, Blok, p. 219.

My letters to the King of Navarre were captured by the people of Toulouse and were sent along with the *Brutum Fulmen* to him [The Pope]. He is looking for a Sicilian (unless he has already found one) who will get rid of me for a reward of two thousand crowns. The man who warned me is a close friend, and begs that I will beware. But the Lord is my strength, whom then shall I fear? Anyway, I have lived for sixty-four years. . . . [1]

Despite his sixty-odd years, which he seemed to regard as a great age, Hotman retained a healthy curiosity for the world. The same letter contains a reference to "a Prussian nobleman, whose name is Schakmann, [who] has lived here for some time near us. . . . I am delighted with his company, for he has seen many countries, among these Ireland, and has told me many memorable things".

The publication of *De Iure Successionis* necessitated a revised edition of *Franco-Gallia,* the fourth, which appeared at Frankfort in 1586. It was increased by six new chapters, besides lesser alterations. In the first edition he had stated rather generally that the ruler has not unlimited power; in the fourth edition he goes into greater detail as to the specific limitations.

Unrestricted power has not been granted to the kings of France by their subjects, so that they cannot be said to be released . . . from all laws (omnibus legibus soluti). . . . We cannot sufficiently stress the precept SALUS POPULI SUPREMA LEX ESTO. . . . I cannot help marvelling at the blunders of those men who . . . when they had read that . . . by passing the lex Regia, the people had granted all its dominion and power to the Emperor, suddenly attribute . . . unlimited power to all kings. . . . If the Roman Emperors did have vast power, is it therefore true that the same power has been granted to

[1] H. to Grynaeus, s. l. 27 November, 1586, in Hummel, B. F., *Celebrium Virorum . . . Epistolae Ineditae,* Nurnberg, 1777, p. 81. The age given does not agree with the accepted date of his birth.

every king by his people? We must not draw a general conclusion from one particular instance.

The system of government of the Poles, Danes, Swedes, and Spanish, was very different from this. Tacitus commented on the freedom of the Germans. The king of England could levy no tribute without the consent of the Orders and Estates. Finally there was no province of France which had not made special compacts before yielding to the king's government.

The first and greatest restriction, then, is that the king must preserve inviolate the authority of the public council; it should be summoned whenever the necessity of the State demands it. Former kings could decide nothing without the consent of the Estates; a survival of this remained at the time of writing, for the Parisian Senate, which had taken over a great part of the power of that former parlament, suffered no decrees or edicts of the king to be registered until they had met with the approval of the councillors.

The next check is the inability of the king to dispose of the kingdom by testament; the succession to the kingdom is determined by the institutions and customs of their ancestors.

The third law flows from the second, and marks an adaptation of the original thesis to fit the special needs of the period. When the king dies, the "hereditas regni" passes on to his eldest born son; the younger son cannot precede him, nor is it permissible for any other to take his place. This is not due to inheritance, but to the common law.

No woman may succeed to the throne, but in the default of direct male heirs, the nearest agnate to the dead king shall take his place, even if he be further removed in relationship than the woman.

The fifth law had been mentioned previously. The king had not right to diminish the domain without the authority of the Estates. In this matter of alienation three things must be considered: Was there no other means of obtaining money? Was the need very great? Was the price suitable?

The privilege exercised by some executives of modern times was denied to the King of France. He could not forgive a crime or remit capital punishment, without parlementary consent.

No magistrate of the realm could be dismissed from office unless the cause was known and approved by the council of Peers.

The eighth law forbade the arbitrary debasement of the coinage. The interests of the entire population were so deeply involved that their consent must be obtained.

In the last chapter, he allows some expression of his personal grievances and adds to the former criticism of Parlement one final burst of fury. France is overrun with pettifoggers and unwanted solicitors. In the days of yore, they had lived at peace. Now a third of the population pursue this profession, and the French people, of all those upon whom the sun shines the most highly endowed in art, letters and religious zeal, spend their days in bickering, scandalmongering, and in fighting law suits, as if they were draining sewers. The multitude of cases blocks the courts so that even those who have just claims must wait an eternity for settlement. The judges are no longer impartial.

Is there any one who can contemplate without weeping the fact that not only the clients and beneficiaries of the Roman pontiff . . . and those endowed with ecclesiastical wealth win over a large proportion of these magistrates, but even those who call themselves laity have sold themselves and their faith . . . to the papal tyranny, for the sake of passing on their possessions to their children.

The source of all this trouble is the baneful influence of Rome.

It is evident that the cause . . . is partly impiety, partly the incredible superstition . . . which like a heavy mist hangs over the whole Christian world, and when the light of Christian faith was extinguished, the sacred Bible hidden away, all things were veiled in the dense shadows of superstition. . . . If through God's goodness the might of the Holy Bible shall prevail again in France, and youth be trained in its study, there is no doubt but that as the shadows vanish at sunrise, so will this pettifogging art, along with the beliefs drawn from the same source, be driven away.

It is of course impossible to divorce completely the incidents of a man's life from his political theory. Hotman had certain ideals for a government in France which would serve his own cause, and the aims of the party to which he belonged. He was perhaps less self-seeking than many others, in that he consciously gave up an inheritance for his faith, although at any moment he could have regained it by recanting.

In its main outlines, his ideal for the state is that of Calvin. When he diverges, he follows a more democratic tangent. But although they would create very similar organisations, nevertheless they start with different theories of the origin of law. Calvin built law or constitutions upon the idea of natural equity, which he felt was common to all peoples; Hotman sees the sanction for law in age-old custom. Therefore to justify his desired form of government, he must prove that it had once existed. Both agreed that the magistrate was the guardian and conservator of the laws, but where Calvin considered him as the vicar of God, Hotman saw him the elect of the people. Neither granted to him indiscriminant use of public funds. Calvin taught passive obedience for individual subjects, unless indeed the prince should make a command in defiance of God. Hotman, like the author of *Vindiciae,* (whom he preceded by six years) felt that resistance to a tyrant was the duty of any group to which the nation collectively had delegated authority.

It has been alleged that Hotman changed his theme from a defense of popular government to the support of dynastic rule, and hence was guilty of contradiction. Surely this criticism is superficial. In 1567 he upheld the constitutional importance of the Estates General,—only incidentally, it is true. In 1573 he published a book on this theme, defending a monarch by election, in which the kingly powers are limited by the original compact with the people, and in which the assembly plays the double role of assistant to the king and watch dog for the people. In 1585 and 1586, he does cease to advocate monarchy by election, but he gives no greater authority to the king thereby. The king is bound by definite traditional precedents, among which is the inability to name his successor. At the death of each incumbent of office, the sovereignty reverts to the nation, just at Hotman had said in 1573, but with this difference, that the nation, instead of selecting among a number of candidates, itself recognises certain well established customs in naming a successor. The assembly holds the same important position under the hereditary constitutional monarchy that it had held under an elective constitutional monarchy. Neither Calvin nor Hotman had extremely democratic views. Both were intellectuals, with something of disdain for the emotional unthinking masses, whom they would not admit to a share in the body politic.

The revision of *Franco-Gallia* contained Hotman's last contribution to the field of political theory. Fortune never dealt kindly with him thereafter; his life was too harassed for continued and creative thought. The move to Geneva had not been a wise one. Basel, Lutheran though it was, offered greater safety. The Duke of Savoy, once vidame for the Bishop of Geneva, was anxious to regain his temporal control of the city. Many roads were cut off; food supplies were scarce and dear. In the summer of 1586 there was another visitation of the plague; winter set in early, with extreme cold; the Rhone was frozen over at Geneva by the first week of December.[1] Hotman had only a very small income, and several daughters to support. In his despair, he turned to alchemy. It is rather pitiful to find a mind once so alert and courageous, groping, in its despair, for the philosopher's stone. He sold his books to buy chemicals for further experiment; at one time he felt that he was on the threshold of success, and wrote in great delight to a friend.[2] Meanwhile other cares were pressing upon him. " . . . The harvest is coming, and then winter; it is time for the father of a family to consider the warming of the hypocaust". The Elector Palatine wrote to the Queen of England, asking aid for the distressed author. Jean Hotman was by this time high in favor with the Earl of Leicester, but no influence could persuade Elizabeth to part with money for so small a cause.

In the summer of 1589 the Savoyards approached so close as to cut off all access by land. In August Hotman tried to flee by boat; in the early autumn he was successful, and wrote from Basel, appealing for funds.

When I noticed . . . . that one exit remained, by way of the lake, although I had been ill in bed for twelve days, nevertheless I threw myself in a boat, and by sailing all night, arrived at Morgias early in the morning. I reached Basel as best I could.

You have now the story of my third ruin: since naked, shipwrecked, needy and almost reduced to beggary, I have fallen for the third time into catastrophe, after two flights and the pillaging of my possessions, which I suffered at Bourges

[1] H. to Bas. Amerbach, s. l. 8 December, 1586, Basel, G II 19, fol. 218.

[2] H. to Zwinger, various letters from Geneva in 1586, Basel, Fr. Gr. Ms. II 28, Nos. 135, 136, 137, 138, 139, 140, 141.

years ago. . . . . This has been my fate, and verily, like the patriarch of old could I say, "My days have been few and evil". But nevertheless I am not broken in spirit, nor will I give myself up to grief and repining, but sustain myself by faith in that felicity which God . . . . has promised us after this wretched life. I know that calamity is the faithful attendant of piety, nor did Christ when he called us to him, promise riches and dignities, but a cross and heavy burdens.[1]

He tried to interest prominent men in schemes for editing books, but they paid no heed, and ill health pursued him. In February of the next year he died of dropsy.

His son went to Basel two years later, to arrange his father's papers. "I find several of his works not yet edited, but we shall publish every thing . . . shortly."[2] Elsewhere he adds

I have made an index of all the books which my father wrote. . . . The work was pleasant, because in one and the same act I was increasing his fame, and rendering a service to the State. But it was a labor in which no one could assist me, for the good old man wrote in such a way that he indicated his thoughts in characters known to me alone.

And again,

In these writings of his I have found several, both in the civil law and in the humane studies. . . . I have now transcribed all these from his manuscript—no small task, for, since no mortal could follow his writing (which consisted entirely in notes and certain abbreviations) or even guess at it, I was forced to undertake this task alone.

It was due indirectly to this filial labor that we have the edition of Lyons, 1599-1600, which comprises three volumes, but not all the writings of Hotman.

[1] To Baron Streimius, 26 October, 1589. Brit. Mus. Harley 4935, vol. 68 E.

[2] J. Hotman to unknown 10 December, 1592. Bibl. Nat., Fonds Latin 8586.

CHAPTER IV

BODIN: THE GOVERNMENT ORGAN

WHEN Jean Bodin (1530?-1596) is mentioned, one is apt to think of La République, and absolutism, but in making that generalisation, one should consider the political theory of his earlier work, the *Methodus,* as well as the special circumstances under which the Republic was written. Certain it is that Bodin had not the impetuous nature of Hotman. He had a cooler head, no less intelligent; little religious ardor, hence greater tolerance of all creeds; less willingness to sacrifice his own interests for a cause worth while; in short, he possessed a large share of prudence, that cardinal virtue which serves so well, but endears so little.[1]

It seems odd that of the two he should have been the shrewder and colder, for he was born in the Loire valley (at Angers), spent in the South the first half of his life, of which twelve years were passed in Languedoc, and did not reach Paris until he was thirty-one. Hotman on the other

[1] Little trace of the personal life of Bodin can be found. The documents, almost all of which were in France, have vanished. Perhaps three or four letters in his handwriting remain. Discovery has been announced very recently of a few additional letters in Picardy. This entire register of a notary at Ham dated back to 1532; unfortunately the larger part was destroyed in the war [See *La Revue du seizième siècle*, XV (1928), 56-99]. Otherwise his career must be followed by means of chance remarks in printed works, or in biographical notices of early writers who had access to material now lost. The difficulty with these secondary sources is that the authors shared in the prejudices of their day, and too often repeated as fact what was only rumour. The excellent critique which was published in 1914 by M. René Chauviré has been followed for the biographical matter stated here.

hand was born in the north of France, of German extraction, and with the exception of a decade, spent all his life in the border regions.

I had selected these two as antitheses: one, a Huguenot, defending self-government; the other, a Romanist, defending absolutism. But as the work progressed, it seemed that the contrast was less clear-cut. Temperamentally, they were far apart. Further than that one might hestitate to say. There can be no doubt as to the principles of Hotman,—he was protestant both in religion and in politics. The only possible ground of dispute would be as to cause and effect: was he republican because he was a Huguenot, or did he join the ranks of the Calvinists to urge on the attack against absolutism? As we read his letters, it seems impossible to believe that he used his faith as a lever for his politics, although this thesis has been asserted for the group as a whole.[1]

It is less easy to diagnose Bodin. He never left the fold of the Roman Church, yet his opinions were so tolerant that his orthodoxy was frequently questioned. Rumours even were spread that his mother had been a Spanish Jewess. Politically he followed the same path of compromise. What he said in days of peace, he retracted in times of stress. This was done partly to consolidate the royal forces in the face of anarchy, as he himself avers,—partly in fear for his own safety, a fact which he does not so readily admit.

His family, so far as can be learned, had held office in Angers, both ecclesiastic and judicial, and must have been of the well to-do middle class. The boy studied law at the University of his native city, where he was sufficiently brilliant to obtain the assistance of the bishop. In 1548 he

[1] F. J. C. Hearnshaw, *Social and Political Theories*, Brentano, N. Y. (n. d.), p. 29.

went to Toulouse for further study, and teaching. We have only slight traces of his occupations there—a quarrel with Cujas, who had awakened the ire of Hotman also: a visit to the provincial Estates of 1566, and a very uncertain visit to Geneva a little earlier. The evidence for this last rests on the fact that one Jean Bodin was enrolled among the citizens of Geneva in 1552. He had intellectual interests in common with many of the Protestant group; in later years he showed a detailed knowledge of Genevese history, and a certain sensitiveness to criticism from that quarter: he was in the service of Alençon, the leader of the party of compromise. But then, compromise was the keynote of his character, and the whole Calvinistic connection remains shadowy. If he did go to Geneva as a young man of twenty-two, it was the one rash act of his life. He soon regretted his expatriation and returned to Toulouse, where for a few years he was professor of Roman law.[1]

Why he moved to Paris in 1561, we do not know, unless he wanted a wider theater for his talents. He practised law privately for six years, apparently with little profit, since in 1567 he accepted an appointment as procureur-general for the king at the Grands Jours of Poitiers.

It would be interesting to know if Bodin and Hotman had come in contact. The latter was in France at this time, in Valence, Bourges, Paris and Orleans. Certain men were known to both of them, notably Charles du Moulin, and Etienne Pasquier, and it is hardly conceivable that they did not meet. The only definite link that I have found is a purely formal letter from Jean Hotman to Bodin, dated Windsor, 1582. Even that may have been the result of Bodin's visit to England in 1581.

The *Methodus ad Facilem Historiarum Cognitionem* appeared in 1566. Its purpose is given in the preface,—to

[1] *De la République* (Cologne, 1608), *Epistola*, no pagination.

explain how one ought to read the best of history, and how, by using this method, one may pluck the most valuable fruits therefrom. Then too, he hoped to "encourage to this most appealing study others who have more leisure, more talent, more knowledge, more judgment" than he. He criticises the historiography then in fashion.

When I came into the forum . . . I proposed this to myself first of all: that all the time which I had free from forensic business, I would spend in appropriate study, and thereby make return . . . in whatever way I could, to the State to which, after immortal God, we owe all things.

But then I noticed that there were three kinds of writing: (1) finding material, and making discoveries, (2) arranging the facts in order, and polishing off the form, (3) removing the errors of former books: it seemed remarkable to me that there are, and always have been, so many authors, but few who arranged their material reasonably and artistically. . . . The more awkward a man is at writing, the greater the number of books he pours forth. . . . Art and knowledge . . . are not separate things, but parts of a whole. . . .

In history the best part of universal law lies concealed. It was this relationship that drew him to the study of history and historiography. His first interest was jurisprudence, but to make adequate preparation for that subject, he felt the necessity of a knowledge of all peoples—not such an account as was too frequently given, a mere assortment of fact,—but an analysis and synthesis which should reveal the underlying philosophy. Through this preliminary study of history, he intended to prepare himself, and others, for that searching inquiry into the laws of nations which seem to have fascinated the humanistic jurists of the sixteenth century. In the preface to the *Methodus* there is the same interest and aim which was expressed in *Antitribonian.* The two books were written almost contemporaneously, and probably derive from the same source, the Chancellor. There is the same contempt for the garbled form of the Roman Code that had descended to them, the same desire to search out the best in the law of every nation—Persian, Greek, Egyptian, Jewish, Spanish, English, German, Turkish. It was an attempt to find unity, or perhaps continuity, in legalistic thought throughout the ages. Bodin claims Plato as his inspiration,

> Plato, who thought that there was one form of propounding laws, and of regulating the state,—if all the laws of all the states, or at any rate of the more famous states, should be collected, and the sages should compare them, and should combine the best of these. To this idea therefore I have directed all my studies and all my thoughts.

To trace the sources of *ius* from its beginning, to grasp clearly the power and authority of prince, senate, people and magistrate, he sought light from history; and though he realised that nothing is more difficult and more nearly divine than accurate analysis, nevertheless, in his first chapter, *Quid Historia sit et quotuplex,* he proceeded to subdivide the whole field into human, natural, mathematical and divine history. Natural history, in the general application of its laws is certain, but because it deals with material objects, is liable to some error. Mathematical history, made up of abstractions, is perfectly definite and certain (certiorem). Human history is confused and uncertain, but the divine is certissima and unchangeable.

The second chapter, discussing arrangement of the facts of history, implies the necessity of perspective and proportion.

The third, which is of considerable importance in the development of his political theory, offers an explanation of human society. History he plans to narrow down to the limited actions of mankind, but since, even with this restriction, there is a vast field to cover, he feels that it is necessary to distribute human interests among different heads. In order properly to understand history, and to retain it in memory when understood, related matter of importance should be arranged in a definite order.

Man's activities are threefold: those which have to do with maintenance of life (*ad tuendam vitam*), those concerning material arts (*ad instituendam*), those dealing with spiritual and cultural interests (*ad cultum*). But since it is difficult, or impossible, for man to obtain single-handed necessities, comforts, or esthetic delight, he seeks society, which is the source of so many advantages. Human activities converge to the maintenance of this institution, by the development of three complementary types of training,—complementary, yet in a sense, each a prerequisite to the next. They are moral, domestic, and civil training, to teach, in turn, self-control, regulation of the household, and political administration.

Civil discipline, of which jurisprudence is but a part, is separated into three parts, imperium, consilium, executio. Advice must be sought from those who share the imperium. There is a distinction between giving law, and giving advice concerning desirable laws. The latter is for the Senate, the former for the people, or the prince, or for those who have control of the state.[1] The actual promulgating of law rests then with the man (or group) who holds the imperium. But he is not an autocrat for he must consult with the Senate with regard to raising or diminishing tribute, to foreign policy, and to commercial activities. All officials are di-

[1] *Methodus*, p. 26. Consilium autem capi solet de iis, in quibus imperium versari diximus. Aliud est enim legem ferre, aliud de lege ferenda consultare. Hoc senatus, illud populi vel principis est, vel illorum qui Reipublicae summam habent.

rected by the authority of him who has command of the state, but the ecclesiastics are not subordinate—they merely assist in state functions. Religion itself needs no outward manifestation; the conscious turning of the cleansed heart toward God can best be achieved in solitude. Indeed the most blessed life is that of contemplation, but since the entire State cannot withdraw itself from worldly affairs, the highest good for a man pursuing a life in the world, must be defined not by retirement, not by absorption in business, but by a mixture of the two, if we wish the supreme good for man and State to coincide.

Chapter five contains the famous climatic theory which Montesquieu is supposed to have borrowed, but Bodin's thought is tinctured so strongly with medievalism, that the two seem very far apart. He has strange notions of physiology, and a mysticism compounded of over-strained analogies. Without trying to probe the depths of this fanciful obscurity, which after all digresses widely from a theory of the State, we might describe this chapter as an attempt to explain the effect of environment upon human life, in order to evaluate the characteristics of the more illustrious races, with a view to obtaining a further insight into their institutions.[1]

In a long chapter entitled "De Statu Rerumpublicarum" he discusses the foundation and development of government, which he considers the proper realm of history. The things

[1] Statuendum nobis . . . quae qualisque sit omnium aut maxime illustrium populorum natura, ut historiarum veritatem iustis ponderibus examinare, ac de rebus singulis rectius iudicare possimus. . . . Quaeramus igitur illa quae non ab hominum institutis, sed a natura ducuntur quaeque stabilia sunt, nec unquam nisi magna vi, aut diuturna disciplina mutantur; et mutata nihilominus ad pristinam redeunt naturam. . . . Quibus intellectis ac perceptis, magnam partem historiarum intellectam perceptamque fore confido. Atque haud scio an ulla disputatio magis ad universam historiarum cognitionem et incorruptum earum iudicium necessaria videatur. *Methodus*, chapter v.

which are gleaned from the reading of historians about the beginning of states, growth, condition, tendency and fall are greatly needed; nothing is more effective for the preservation of human society, than to be informed in the science of directing the State. The ancients have written well and worthily upon this subject, although they were not agreed as to the best type of state. Twelve hundred years after darkness had covered everything, Machiavelli contributed a political discussion which became very famous, but his work would have been better and nearer to the truth if he had known the ancients. There were others like Patricius and Sir Thomas More, but they place before our eyes, just as if it were history, pure fiction of states, without attaching any system thereto.

Dismissing thus the Utopian type of commonwealth, he plans a more practical investigation, building up his state, not from ideals or desires, but by a comparison of all the important empires that had existed, so that the universal state might be more easily comprehended. Thence we can understand what laws are necessary in a kingdom, likewise those suited to a popular or an aristocratic state. Although he plans to use the opinions of philosophers and historians, he refers chiefly to Aristotle, at any rate for definition of terms used: citizen, state, republic, magistrate, imperium. But he refers only to disprove.

Aristotle defines a citizen as one who has the right to share in office, trials, and public counsel. Bodin points out that this is too narrow, since it applies only to the citizen of a popular state, whereas a definition should cover universals. He replaces it by an explanation founded on the analogy between family life and membership in a state,—a citizen is one who enjoys the common liberty and protection of authority. If one reasons from the probable course of family life in the era of Bodin, this would give the citizen civil liberty, but no voice in government.

The Aristotelian Republic is the sum of the collectivity of citizens with the body of magistrates (*descriptionem civitatis et magistratuum*). Bodin objects to this because it assumes the prior existence of the civitas (as a component) to the Respublica, an assumption which, in its turn, would imply that the civitas was a group of men without magistrates and imperium.

But if several should come together in one spot without laws or rule,—if no one considers the common property, which does not exist, but if each looks after his private affairs,—if there are no punishments for the wicked, no reward for the good, how then can the image of the civitas exist? Therefore this collected multitude ought not to be called civitas, but anarchy, or by some other name than civitas, since men of this sort are . . . without law.[1]

For Bodin, the true image of a Republic is the family or the college; and as a family cannot consist of one man, so a Republic cannot consist of one family. If several live under the same roof, without appointed commander, the group cannot endure. But husband, wife, children and servants are kept together by the private authority of the father. It does not matter whether they live in one spot or not, for they are joined together by lawful and restrained rule. So is a Republic the fusion of several families, even though widely separated, if only they are under the protection of the same rule. Either one commands all, or all command the different members, or a few command the group. Contrary to the Aristotelian theory the size of the republic does not affect

[1] Bodin's distinction between civitas and respublica is not so clear as Aristotle's. Does he want to define civitas as the collectivity of citizens *under the same sovereignty?* If so, then civitas and Respublica are either complementary (non-existent one without the other) or else they are two different ways of looking at the same thing. In either case, what about the third element, the magistrates?

its classification, and Geneva or Rhagusa is no less a republic than the empire of the Tartars. It is not essential that all the citizens of a state should be living under the same system of law; the only test is the sharing of the same magistrates and authority.

A magistrate, according to Aristotle, is one who has authority, jurisdiction, and the right of sharing in counsel. This does not satisfy Bodin, for few magistrates are admitted to the public council, and none has imperium. This would be possible only if the sovereign had shorn itself of its chief attribute. Magistrates have, it is true, a certain delegated share of authority, which is confined to the issuance of decrees, and the application of statute law.

The highest power, which involves the majesty and the type of State, is rendered variously as τὸ κυρίον πολίτευμα, *signoria, souveraintê, summa rerum* and *summum imperium.* Upon the nature of this concept depends the solution of many obscure problems about the Republic, yet Aristotle and other important writers have evaded it. The *summa rerum* consists in five parts; the first and principal, in the creation of magistrates, and in defining their power; the next in promulgating or abrogating the laws; the third in declaring war and peace; the fourth in supreme jurisdiction; the last in the power of life and death, since the law itself leaves no excuse for clemency. If these are the aspects of the Sovereign, how we may explain their occasional exercise by mere magistrates? Has the magistrate "pure" authority, or does it reside in the Prince alone? Has the authority actually been transferred to the magistrate, thereby depriving the Prince, or does he still retain all of his power while permitting its exercise by a deputy? If it is true that no magistrate can hand on his power, then obviously it is only an emanation from the Prince. This leads Bodin to a discussion of the relationship between the action of the law, and the function of the judge.

There are two heads of universal justice (JUS), law and equity, upon which legal action depends, and which affect also the duties of the magistrate. Whatever relation the law has to its action, that same relation equity has to the function of the magistrate. When a decision is to be rendered according to law, the magistrate may not delegate his powers. He can move only within the limits of the law, which practically decide the case for him. But in his equitable jurisdiction, he may hand on cases to others. Many civil suits cannot be entirely covered by statute law, for there is an infinity; they are not bound by the action of the law, but are settled by the magisterial sense of justice. Under these circumstances judges may decide many things beyond the law, or even occasionally against the law; they may correct, or bend, mitigate or aggravate the law, by giving forth decrees.

Therefore the office of magistrate is dual; in respect of action of law, it is a salaried office, since he merely carries out the commands of the law. As he has only a mandate, he may not pass this over to another, but when his term of office is ended, the honors and powers which he has temporarily held, must return to the donor. In his equitable capacity, however, where he is not held strictly to law, there is no mandate, and since he may exercise discretion, he has authority—in a limited sphere—which he may delegate.

Attributes which pertain to the Senate or magistrates have a quality distinct from sovereignty, otherwise sovereignty exists in those who have received it from others. This produces an absurdity parallel to that of the mixed state, where the sovereignty is assumed to exist partly in the people, partly in the Senate, partly in the executive. Such a division of sovereignty seems to Bodin indefensible and indeed impossible. He contends that in Rome the sovereignty rested with the people; in Florence, after the dregs of the plebs had been disenfranchised, laws were proclaimed and magistrates created by the people. In the three types of republic which he recognises, the ultimate authority rests with people or optimates or monarch. It is never shared. The decrees of the Senate always require the sanction of the Prince, whether he be unique or multiple.

Having analysed the quality of the *summa rerum*; having denied the possibility of its division among the various branches of government, he concludes that we may easily identify the type of state by determining who ultimately creates the magistrates and proclaims law. When the *summa rerum* is in the hands of one man, this state is a monarchy, but of monarchies there are two types, absolute and constitutional. The empires of ancient days would comprise the former group. Bodin is not entirely certain how nearly absolute this power should be, but seems to cogitate as he writes, arguing first on the one side, then the other. He agrees that all magistrates must keep within the law, in so far as law can cover the emergency. But he is faced with an obvious difficulty. Conditions are not static; law must change. If all, even the Sovereign, must respect the law, how then is any alteration to take place? Those who give law ought to be above the law; in order that they may abrogate, alter, or even dispense with the law." Having issued this program of absolutism, he mitigates it by adding,

It sounds very fine, that he who gives the laws ought to be superior to them . . . but once the law has been passed, and approved by consent of all, why should not the prince be held by this law which he has promulgated? . . . Therefore if it is fair that whatever each man lays down against another, should hold for him also, how much the more fair is it that prince and people should be bound by its own laws.[1]

[1] *Methodus*, p. 203. Honesta quidem oratio est, oportere legibus su-

It is sophistry to say that the Prince is *legibus solutus,* yet most of the ancient rulers appear to have ignored the law, and to have conducted themselves as masters of all things. Even this would not be contrary to nature, provided that they watch over the republic as would the father over a family.

The other type is of those who limit themselves by the accepted laws. In this group are included nearly all Christian princes, who, when they are crowned, take a great oath, and bind themselves to govern justly according to the laws of the realm.[1] Nor, having sworn, can the monarch easily violate his faith, for the same thing is right for him as for a private citizen, and he is held by the same laws. The king of France cannot destroy the laws of the country, nor change anything of the habits of the citizens or ancient customs, without the consent of the three Estates. "It is clear . . . that Aristotle was mistaken, when he writes that those kings who were bound by law were not kings. If they have the sovereignty, of course they are kings."[2]

Jurisconsults are mistaken in applying to princes the words of Ulpian about the Roman emperors—that they were not only freed from the laws, but that their very will was law. Jaso basely stated before Louis XII that all things belong to the prince, an interpretation which is averse to the cus-

periorem esse, qui legem iubet, propter ea quae diximus: sed lege lata, summoque omnium probata consensu, cur non teneatur princeps, ea lege, quam tulit? . . . Igitur si aequum est ut quod quisque iuris in alium statuit, eodem ipse teneatur; quanto est aequius Principem aut populum suis legibus obligari?

[1] *Ibid.*, p. 204. Formula initiationis regum nostrorum . . . pulcerrima visa mihi est . . . quod Princeps iurat se omnibus ordinibus debitam legem ac iustitiam redditurum . . . neque vero iuratus fidem violare facile potest aut si possit, nolit . . . ius enim illi dicitur ut privato cuique et iisdem legibus tenetur.

[2] For Bodin, sovereignty consists of the five points mentioned on p. 91.

toms and laws of the realm of France. Bodin quotes from Seneca a phrase which Hotman also used, to show that while the king may have possession in a universal sense, "potestas omnium", nevertheless the separate units are the property of the individual subject.

Societies were formed originally through a need for protection and justice. At that time the full liberty of all, the privilege of living without laws or control, was abandoned and command was handed over to one man, who was created leader that his subjects might enjoy justice. When the French king is crowned, he swears to maintain justice, so that this seems to be the chief cause of his creation. Therefore the first type of republic must have been a monarchy. It may have been founded on justice without any laws, dependent entirely on the equity of the prince, or it may have been the rule of a powerful man accompanied by a band of robbers. Those early kingdoms alternated between an equitable rule and a tyranny. Bodin finds no trace of aristocracy, or democracy, until later times, and then only "in the middle region sloping west". Their appearance in Europe is due to the fact that men of the temperate climate are born for the management of affairs, and think themselves worthy of rule; because they excel the easterners in greatness of spirit, they cannot easily endure tyranny. On that account they either force the kings themselves to obey the laws ("than which nothing can be more divine") or they set up the rule of people or nobles.

The most ancient law of France is the Salic, which debars women from succession to the throne. Another fundamental restriction is the Agrarian law, whereby the public lands are protected from alienation without the consent of all others. Furthermore, no decision of the king is binding unless it is in keeping with equity and truth,[1] for it would be

[1] Ex omnibus tamen imperii legibus nulla sanctior est, quam quae vetat

rejected by the magistrates. The superior courts really have no system of laws except those which they approve by registration, but unfortunately this custom is lapsing. The king may not deprive any one of an office, unless he shall have been convicted of crime and condemned in a public trial. It is a moot question whether a magistrate should have a long or short term of office. Bodin advocates life tenure in a kingdom, otherwise the magistrates would not form an effective deterrent upon the prince. What would they dare against his desires, when they feared for their honors? A short term is bad in other respects, for we do not easily obey, nor with dignity command, those with whom we associate daily. Then, too, by a frequent change of magistrates,[1] the power of the prince is increased, until it threatens to become tyranny. But the more one takes away from the power of the prince, the more just the authority is and the more stable it will become. It is a matter of great importance to keep the prince-ship within the power of the laws.

Nature herself has decreed that monarchy is the best form of government, for a similar scheme exists in every type of living thing. How absurd to share the sovereignty among all the citizens! To provide riches in equal amounts was not so unwise as to divide the authority, because each can enjoy his own wealth, but foresight in ruling is by nature yielded to few. For what can be more stupid than the plebs? What more intemperate? And when it becomes inflamed against good people, what more frenzied? Since it is impossible to entrust the government to the foolish plebs, it

principum rescriptis ullam rationem haberi, nisi aequitate perinde ac veritati consentanea sint: quo sit ut pleraque a magistratibus respuantur. . . . Saepe enim audita vox est magistratuum, Nihil posse principem contra leges. *Methodus*, p. 258.

[1] In frequenti magistratuum mutatione principis potestas omnium maxime augetur . . . aucta tyrannis evadit. At quo plus detraxeris imperio principis . . . eo iustius est imperium ac stabilius futurum. *Ibid.*, p. 261.

must be limited to the wisest, the optimates, or since it is easier to find one wise man than many, to the prince. He should be an hereditary ruler, not elective, for there is great danger to the state in interregna, and he must be carefully educated. Of all the things that are discussed about laws and states, nothing is worthy of greater stress than that the prince should understand that he has come into the world for the true cult of God. This is the very foundation of the State, without which it is useless to enact laws against the princely power, for what magistrate, what laws, what authority will coerce him, unless he is checked by religious scruple?

This closes chapter six, and brings to an end his discussion of government. There are four more chapters, covering such matters as a refutation of those who maintain the existence of a golden age, and a system of establishing national origins based on language and geographic situation.

In resuming the work as a whole, one recognises two contributions, a philosophy of history which is new, and a political theory, which, while its foundation is the absolutism of ancient times, nevertheless betrays the sixteenth century in its conception of the nationalist state, and its concentration upon problems of government distinct from relations with the Church. Bodin's interest in history is of course secondary to his interest in politics, but his comparative method, with its preliminary analysis and its ultimate generalisation, was original and fruitful. He was original also in building his theory upon the acts of fairly recent history (The Empire, Spain, England, and so forth) although as a jurist he could not of course ignore the Romans. It was an inductive method,—the integration of known things, to reach a general conclusion, portraying a state which had some claim to reality, rather than an ideal which ought to exist, but did not.

His generalised State is distinctly monist. It is an entity higher than the collectivity of citizens " to whom, after God, we owe all things ". It could hardly be otherwise, given his premises for the foundation of states: one theory is creation by force,[1] the other is by compact, but by a compact of that type with which the name of Hobbes is associated, where, for the sake of protection, the full liberty of all is handed over to one man by separate individuals.

Sovereignty is manifested in the five attributes mentioned on a previous page. There are others, and all are merely symptoms of an inherent quality which apparently defies description. Bodin reproaches Aristotle for avoiding the issue, yet he himself does not define sovereignty, although he names it in four different languages. This intangible, unanswerable will-to-be-obeyed may rest with prince, optimates or people, according to the type of state. For him the monarchy is the best of all possible types, through conformity and reason, therefore sovereignty is the attribute of the king, and flows down from him to the magistrates. Thus far it is absolutism pure and simple. But either he was frightened at the goal to which this chain of logic would lead, or else he was not sincere in his convictions as to the legal supremacy of the monarch, for he turns at right angles, to argue the superiority of a monarchy in which the king is bound by the very law that he has just made. Nature will permit him to be a paternal despot, but it is for the good of all that he should submit to be bound by the checks which his wisdom has imposed upon his subjects. Bodin had in mind Louis IX and Edward I; perhaps thereafter he suddenly thought of Philip IV and Edward II. Absolutism has precedent to build upon, but constitutional monarchy,—if we may call it that—is a desideratum. Constitutional in the modern sense is not an exact rendering of Bodin's general

[1] *Methodus*, p. 155.

conclusions, for his king would promulgate law with the advice of the Council. This body had no veto power, and the people are not considered. In fact, a monarchy where the king listens to the voice of the people is not a monarchy for Bodin, but a democracy. Nevertheless, he recognises the dangers of concentration of power by affirming that the greater the check on the king, the more stable will his authority become.

Insofar as he delineates the French government, he specifies several definite restrictions upon royal prerogative, and regrets the weakening of one of them. At the time of his accession, the king swears to govern justly and to recognise the fundamental laws. Of these, at least three seriously impair his sovereignty, or rather destroy his claim to sovereignty, since one flaw is sufficient to vitiate that all inclusive abstraction. He may not use the land as though it were his own; he may not embody into law any wish of his heart, for Parlement will refuse those inequitable; he may not change any ancient customs, without the consent of the Three Estates.[1]

One might almost say that in France Bodin thought he had found his ideal government realised, for in the general discussion he had emphasised the superiority of a monarchy over the other types of states, and had depicted the king as the fountain-head whence all power flowed. At the same time he pleads for limitations upon that all-pervading privilege—"at quo plus detraxeris imperio principis . . . eo justius est imperium ac stabilius futurum".[2] And again " [Westerners] cannot easily endure tyranny. Wherefore they either force the kings themselves to obey the laws . . .

[1] Leges autem totius imperii proprias convellere non potest... nec de moribus civitatum et antiqua consuetudine quicquam immutare sine trium ordinum consensu. *Methodus*, p. 136.

[2] *Ibid.*, p. 261.

or they drive the tyrants from the throne."[1] Is it not exactly this situation which he describes in France? The king is the most important feature of the government, a beneficent, fatherly ruler, who has sworn at the altar to maintain justice. There is a medieval strain in the popular attitude of love and veneration, something of divine right resulting from the vow to the Deity,—and yet a distinctly earthly and modern set of restrictions is placed upon the king. It is not only moral law by which he is bound; there are perfectly definite regulations about the domain, about the succession, about the dismissal of officers, about the customs of the realm, and the machinery for the enforcement is human and legal intervention. In one instance he even concedes the election of some of the earlier Capetians.[2] He paints a picture of " the detestable arts of a tyrant ", and so contrives to convey a criticism of conditions in the court of Catherine.

They distribute honors and rewards to foreigners . . . . they secretly sow discord among the nobles and plebs, then they fill the fisc from their injuries and murders . . . . they think up new offices and honors, and offer these for a price, that they may have many bound to them. They appoint thieves and criminals for public office, and for the collection of revenue, so that they sap the people's resources and blood.[3]

In 1566, then he looked upon the French king as the source and embodiment of all power, and at the same time as the first servant of the state. Thus far he maintains consistency, but when he introduces fundamental laws, other than those of nature, when he brings in a legislative veto

[1] *Methodus*, p. 217.

[2] *Methodus*, p. 292. Extat . . . in bibliotheca Bellovisia regis initiandi et eligendi a populo forma vetus, qua dicitur Henricus I apud nos electus esse.

[3] *Methodus*, p. 219.

upon royal bills[1] or a Parlementary veto[2] upon royal ordinances, he is either limiting his sovereign, or dividing the sovereignty. In either case he is producing for France a form of government approaching the constitutional.

The greater glory of his more elaborate work of ten years later has eclipsed the *Methodus,* so that the change in his sentiments during that decade had not been sufficiently marked. There are companion passages in the two books which are absolutely contradictory.

In his official activities, Bodin was zealous in supporting what he felt were fundamental laws, even when the king wished otherwise. In 1571, he was sent, as procureur du roi, to regulate a matter concerning the royal forests in Normandy, where certain lands had been alienated without payment of the tax on sales. Bodin insisted that the title was invalid, since the king did not have the right to sell property that was not his own, but domain land, of which he had merely the usufruct. In the interests of peace Charles IX had to restrain the activities of his too zealous agent.

In the autumn of this same year, Bodin entered the service of d'Alençon, the king's younger brother, as maître des requêtes, and remained affiliated to him until the death of the duke in 1584. He seems to have been in Paris during the massacre of 1572, but later moved to Laon, where in 1576, at the age of forty-six, he married (with his customary prudence) a wealthy widow, whose brother held a post to which Bodin aspired. This he actually inherited, a few years later.

The Politiques, of whom Damville was the actual commander in the field, had created as their sovereign body an assembly composed of three delegates from each province under the army's control. It is interesting to observe that,

[1] See footnote, p. 122.

[2] See footnote, p. 118.

of these three, one was from the nobility, and *two* from the Third Estate. The executive, Damville, could take no action without the consent of this body, which included members of both faiths. They had thus put into operation a system of semi-popular government that had been successful, during its short period of trial, for both administrative and financial purposes, and they were therefore anxious to create a similar machinery for all of France. The peace treaty of May, 1576, contained a provision for an immediate summons of the Estates General. Henry III had no thought of complying with this clause of the treaty, but events moved too rapidly for him.

The same treaty which granted to the Politiques governmental concessions yielded toleration to the Huguenots, and certain fortified places as surety. The terms were in fact so generous that the ultramontanists became alarmed, and in their turn formed a third party, antagonistic to each of the others. Their objectives were unity in religion (remettre . . . le saint service . . . selon la forme et la manière de la sainte Église catholique, apostolique et romaine), support of the king, who should, however, observe his coronation oath, and respect the powers of the Estates (ne rien faire au préjudice de ce qui sera ordonné par les États), and restoration of the former liberties of the provincial Estates. This program might have unified the Church, but it would have decentralised the government. On that score, the Catholics were suggesting a federation very like that which the Politiques has created for the South, with a similar subordination of king to general assembly. Their fidelity to the Roman Church had won the assistance of Philip of Spain,—a rather dubious advantage. The Politiques, on the other hand, had asked and obtained the intervention of the German princes; the king and his mother had their Swiss guards, their Italian favorites. Probably the only reason why they did not engage foreign armies was that they no longer had money to pay them. All the revenues were in the hands of Italian tax-farmers. It was an unedifying spectacle, whether the cause was shortsighted ambition, or religious bigotry, or a lack of any policy whatsoever. However fluctuating and opportunist the monarchy, the other two parties were unconsciously working towards the same goal—a constitutional check upon the sovereign power. Their religious differences had driven them to this stand; royal indecision had made it inevitable; could they have reached a working agreement on the administration of the two religions, it would have been possible, in the weakness of the central power, to raise the Estates General to the position for which during more than two hundred years it had been striving,—beside the king, as an essential factor of the government. It was a fatal blunder to allow the monarchy to play the role of arbitrator between them—to allow the buoyant personality of a Bearnese prince to shackle war-weary subjects with the gilded chains of a benevolent despotism. In former years, the strength of the central government had varied directly as the strength of character of the incumbent of the throne. Louis XV and Louis XVI could not have been absolute kings in the fifteenth or sixteenth centuries; their moral weakness would have occasioned restlessness on the part of nobles or Estates. But the fate of France was decided by 1594. A passion for religious conformity and an impatience against spiritual control, arrayed in opposition, had postponed for another two hundred years the popular government to which both aspired.

In the face of disaffection and bankruptcy Henry III issued letters of convocation for the Estates, hoping to obtain sufficient funds to tide over the emergency, and at the same time to introduce discussions which should antagonise the

Protestants and the moderate Catholics, thereby splitting the party of compromise. The letters, which were sent out in August, 1576, were addressed to the seneschals and baillis of the kingdom, likewise to the governors of the provinces, and to a few great lords. Instructions were to convoke, at the sound of the trumpet, and by public order or otherwise, and to assemble in the square before the church all those of the three estates

> pour conférer et communiquer ensemble tant des remonstrances, plaintes et doléances, que moyens et avis qu'ils auront à proposer à l'assemblée générale de nosdits États: et ce fait, élire, choisir, et nommer un d'entre eux de chacun ordre qu'ils enverront et sera present audit jour 15 novembre en notre ville de Blois, avec amples instructions et pouvoirs suffisantes pour, selon les bonnes, anciennes et louables coutumes de ce royaume, nous faire entendre de la part desdits états tant leurs dites plaintes et doléances que ce qui leur semblera tourner au bien public.[1]

On this occasion, as in 1560, inhabitants of the countryside were invited to take part. One agricultural laborer actually sat in the assembly at Blois. The electoral district was the bailliage, but as the towns alone in previous centuries had had the privilege of sending deputies for the Third Estate, they were now unwilling to be included in the bailliage, lest they should lose their predominance. Paris, Marseilles and Rouen succeeded in retaining their deputies. For the most part, however, the Estates were made up of representatives of the bailliages.

The primary assembly was composed of the male inhabitants of the village, or town. One or two delegates having been selected, a written statement of the wishes of the community was entrusted to their keeping, whereupon they

[1] Quoted in Charleville, *Les États Généraux de 1576* (Paris, 1901), p. 23.

journeyed on to the nearest town of appellate jurisdiction. Here in company with the delegates of other towns of the same district, they made a digest of all the complaints and requests. The cahier of Avallon, for instance, bemoaned the excessive taxation, and asked that decisions made at the request of the Estates should be irrevocable. Furthermore, there should be a regular meeting of the assembly every third year.[1] This secondary group sent delegates to the general assembly of the whole district.

Meanwhile, the chief town of the bailliage had been carrying forward similar measures, but as it had a much larger population to handle, delegates were asked from the various professions (corps et métiers) as well as from the different sections of the town. These met with the town councillors and the local justices to draw up the cahier and elect representatives for the general assembly of the bailliage.

Delegates of the clergy and of the nobility joined the Tiers at this general meeting, but each order deliberated on its separate cahier. Many of the deputies, particularly among the nobility, were royal functionaries, and hence scarcely in a position to take an independent stand against the king. The bailli presided over the general assembly, which elected a member for each order to go to Blois. Occasionally there was more than one member for each order, a perfectly fair arrangement, for the voting was not by head, but by bailliages. Probably the expense accounts, which were borne by the district, prevented an undue exercise of this privilege.[2]

Just what were the qualifications for holding office we do

[1] Archives de la ville d'Avallon AA 37, quoted in Charleville, p. 47.

[2] Note: This account applies only to the provinces which were under the direct control of the king's agent. Sections like Languedoc, where the provincial estates had retained extensive powers, frequently permitted their delegates to be nominated by the Estates.

not know, but there seems to have been at least a semblance of universal responsibility. A free expression of opinion among the illiterate of course could not be seriously considered, but all inhabitants of village or town apparently were entitled to be present at the appointment and to make themselves heard, if they could. Only one Protestant deputy made his appearance at Blois. The Huguenots loudly proclaimed that intimidation had been practised at the elections by royal troops. It strains credulity rather far to think that a small army could have spread itself over so wide a range. More probably, the Huguenots, recognising the hopelessness of contesting the elections, felt that a vociferous minority on the outside, questioning the legality of the elections, would be more effective than a defeated minority which has shared in them.

The deputy had delegated authority to follow certain definite lines of policy. This mandate was expressed in the instructions issued to him; beyond those instructions he could not go. If unexpected events should alter the course of business (such as the sudden death of the king in 1560), they must return to consult the source of their authority. In addition to the private instructions he carried the cahier de doléances, and papers establishing the validity of his election—"les pouvoirs".

Once arrived at Blois, the deputies might assemble to verify their powers, appoint a secretary, and arrange the order of business, but until the king summoned them before him, the meeting had not officially opened. Usually the Tiers voted by bailliages; they would meet at the home of the eldest member of their group for discussion while awaiting the king's arrival. In 1576 they deviated from this arrangement, and voted according to governments. There was an established order of precedence; Paris was given the first place, and was represented by the prévôt des marchands.

After the vote of the Parisian delegate had been cast, the opportunity passed to the next deputy from the Ile de France.

The Journal of Bodin, who had been sent by Vermandois, in which is situated Laon, is a day-to day account of the assembly. He magnifies his own rôle with a childish vanity but incidentally draws a vivid picture of the Estates in action:

On the twenty-fourth [of November] in all the squares of the town was heard the cry, "In the king's name". Each man was told to meet with his order at two o'clock . . . the clergy at the church of St. Sauveur, the nobles at the palace, the Third Estate at the townhall.[1]

They duly met, and were summoned to present themselves in the order maintained at Orleans, when their names were noted in writing. That same afternoon the Archbishop of Embrun visited the nobles and the Third, to invite them to sit together in one house—an offer which they refused.

The first of December, there was a great to-do between the deputies of the Île de France, and the deputies of Burgundy, because Bodin, deputy of Vermandois, and next in succession after the deputies . . . . of the city of Paris, claimed that he followed after the Parisian delegation.

On Monday, the third, the members grouped together by governments to verify their powers. When this was done

Versoris opened the cahier of the city of Paris, where were read the articles on religion, by which it was asked that the king might please to unite all of his subjects in one religion, the Roman Catholic. [It will be remembered that only one Protestant deputy was present at the Estates, and he was

[1] [J. Bodin] *Recueil de tout ce qui s'est négotié en la compagnie du Tiers Estat de France . . . au xv novembre, 1576* (s. l. 1577).

among the nobles.] . . . Bodin, deputy from Vermandois, read the first and twelfth articles of their cahier, which asked that it might please the king to maintain his subjects in peace, and within two years to hold a general or national council, to settle the matter of religion.[1]

Versoris interrupted him, but after dinner the discussion was resumed. Finally it was concluded that the Edict of Pacification should stand, "par douces et saintes voyes". On the fifth of December, the Third Estate sent an envoy to the king, to supplicate that he would receive them separately and honorably, so that they should in no sense seem inferior to the other two orders.

On the seventh, they supplicated the king, with the consent of the other estates, that requests which were made by the Estates, either jointly or severally, should be drawn up into law by a committee formed of one deputy of each order from each government, and of a number of judges appointed by the king who were acceptable to the Estates. Such laws should be irrevocable. Further, they asked for a list of the privy councillors.[2] In the case that a unanimous decision be reached by the three houses, it should automatically become law without further consideration by king or council. The author of this suggestion, which made the Estates sovereign over the king, did not dare let his name be known, but left an anonymous request on the table. On this same day Versoris was elected spokesman for the Third Estate before the king. Henry III temporised. He sent the list of privy councillors, and promised to hear the thirty-six deputies, but reminded them that they could have no vote (voix déliberative). He refused to concede in advance whatever unani-

[1] *Ibid.*, p. 9. *Recueil de pièces originales et authentiques concernant la tenue des Etats Généraux* (Paris, 1789), vol. ii, p. 74. (From an original MS. in the library of M. de Brunville.)

[2] *Recueil de pièces*, vol. ii, p. 195.

mous requests they might proffer, for he could not foresee what demands might be made. There were complaints of the multiplicity of offices created by the king, particularly of the unwieldy size of the privy council. He was petitioned to dismiss all of the group then in power, and to appoint not more than twenty-four, excluding the princes.

Religious toleration was brought forward again. Seven governments favored the enforcement of the Roman Catholic religion, "par les meilleures et plus sainctes voyes and moyens que faire se pourroit", asked that practice of any other religion, either in public or in private, be forbidden, and that ministers, deacons, and other Calvinist leaders be invited to leave the country, notwithstanding edicts to the contrary. The five other governments dissented, on the ground that this change should be brought about by methods gentle and pacific, without warfare. They were voted down, but Bodin comments that one of the dissenting provinces (Guyenne) had 17 deputies, whereas a supporting province (Provence) had but two. If they had followed the usual custom of voting by bailliage, presumably the decision would have supported the peace party. Several defeated deputies from the south-west asked for demission papers, but were refused. "Il y eut grandes altercations et plaintes des cinq governemens susdits."

On this same day, the Bishop of Autun came to the lodging of Bodin, deputy, and revealed to him that several gentlemen had recommended that he should go to the Prince of Condé as emissary for the Third Estate, with the Bishop of Autun, and Montmorin for the nobles. Bodin told him that he was not inclined to such a voyage, in consideration of the severe winter; then too he was of the peace party, and people might be suspicious of him. In any case he had no horses, nor means to buy them. The Bishop of Autun promised him to lend him everything he needed, but Bodin did not care to accept.[1]

[1] *Recueil de tout ce qui s'est passé*... p. 29.

This seems to have been a scheme to be rid of a troublesome speaker, who might interfere with the wishes of the extreme ultramontane group. Bodin remained firmly at Blois.

The first president of the Chambre des Comptes visited the Assembly, sent by the king to explain the state of the finances and the debts contracted by his predecessors, which amounted to more than 100,000,000 livres. A special commission of twelve persons was appointed to meet with the first president, while the other went ahead with the general cahier. They found it impossible to obtain definite information with regard to income and expenditure, for the official would give only summary accounts whose accuracy was questioned. The deputy des Avenelles, a member of the delegation, reported to the main body that certain revenues were being paid to the king which had been appropriated for debts coming due. This amounted to about 7,000,000 livres.

A little later a request was made that they should aid the necessities of the king in view of the possibility of civil war. The royal representatives hoped especially for assistance from those provinces which had asked for uniformity in religion. Whereupon a member from Bordeaux rose up "without commission from his delegation, and out of turn, since he was fourth in order of precedence", and said that in asking for the Roman Catholic religion, they were not supporting war, but hoping that this unification might be brought about a Council, by reforming abuses, and in other ways. The king suggested the elimination of aides and gabelles, and the substitution of a duty to be paid on each fireside, the highest individual tax being fifty livres, the smallest, twelve pence. It was hoped to obtain 15,000,000 livres by this means. The deputies pleaded insufficient powers, and the king was much annoyed. He was discontented chiefly with the deputies from the Ile de France, because he was persuaded that some, egged on by his enemies, were making trouble among the others. He ordered them to take under advice straightway the matter of the two millions cash which he required for six months, and the duty of 15,000,-000 aforesaid and " ne chercher excuse sur leurs procurations ".

The deputy from Auxerre asked the President [prévôt des marchands] . . . why the king laid all the blame on the Ile de France. The President told him that he had heard mention only of Bodin . . . . who was manipulating the others . . . . whereas the said Bodin was thinking only of the good of the people, and the other ten deputies of the Ile de France followed his advice, so that the President of the Third Estate, prévôt des marchands of Paris, and deputy of the same city, was forced to speak according to the opinion of the other deputies of the Ile de France, which was the first government, and whose policy was frequently followed by the others.

This was the reason why the deputies of Paris, to whom Bodin was always opposed when it was a question of public weal, spread various tales about Bodin in the king's hearing —to the effect that

he was opposed to the royal interests. . . . Bodin frequently dined at the king's table, if his official duties did not hinder him, and . . . the king made him talk about the events and stories which were current, as he had done since the twenty-fifth of November, when the king sent for him, and in the presence of several gentlemen, honored him with a command to be present at dinner. . . . The king could not refrain from saying, when they spoke disparaging words about Bodin, that he was a worthy man.[1]

The deputies from Paris " were moving heaven and earth " to obtain for the king the money demanded. Their anxiety was due to an apprehension that in case of war, the

[1] *Recueil de tout ce qui s'est passé* . . . 2nd page 59 (pagination incorrect).

government would appropriate the funds destined for interest payments on municipal obligations. This might have caused a riot in the city, not without danger for their own persons. They therefore tried to put the burden on the rest of France, "faisans bon marché du bien d'autruy". A notice was posted on the door of the assembly room, stating that Paris should supply any necessary funds, since it was she who had plunged France into civil war. After that time the prévôt des marchands came but rarely to the meetings, and Bodin presided in his stead.

On the twelfth of March, deputies from the clergy and the nobles invited the Tiers to select twelve members to confer with an equal number of their representatives over the cahiers, before they were taken to the king. Bodin was sent as spokesman. After a few graceful opening remarks, he introduced a political maxim—that there was nothing more dangerous in matters of State than to be consistent and unyielding; it was better to change, and to adapt one's self to the wisest plans. He admitted that after long thought he had reversed his opinion with regard to the deliberative committee of 36 deputies from the Estates, and his order would supplicate His Majesty to summon no one of them to consult on the cahiers, since the Estates did not have such powers. It was not permitted to a simple procureur to find a substitute, much less to a deputy, who had a public responsibility of such consequence. Even if they had had power to name certain members for consideration of the cahiers, they ought not to do so, in view of the risk which they would incur for the people of France, who were reduced already to four hundred deputies in the Estates; to go further and select from these eighteen or thirty-six would be to minimise their force. Even granting that there was not a man in the group who could be bribed, nevertheless there was a danger that they might be intimidated in the presence of royalty.

Further, though they might be incorruptible and invariable, " nevertheless the decision rests with the king, in the presence of whom all power of privy councillors, magistrates and royal officers cease ". The other two Estates still insisted upon the formation of this committee, and threatened to act independently of the Tiers. Bodin replied that the Third Estate had several complaints to make against the others, and that it was against all human and divine law that they should be both judge and party; the ancient custom of the kingdom retained throughout all Christendom, was that two Estates could do nothing to the prejudice of the third.[1]

That same day, the archbishop of Lyons, who was a former friend of Bodin, inquired why he had taken so extreme a stand. Bodin told him frankly that he would do well to avoid naming the deputies, for the reasons already mentioned, and for others which he could not declare in public. The clergy eventually did not send a committee, thereby annoying the nobles, who said that Bodin manipulated the Estates as he pleased. The king no longer regarded him so favorably, for he put a stumbling block in the way of every plan. Someone suggested that money could be raised by mortgaging a part of the domain, but here again he dissented. Common opinion reckoned the king as merely a life tenant of demesne lands. Their proceeds should be expended, first on the living expenses of His Majesty, then on the salaries of the officials. Any surplus after that should go to public affairs, for the proprietorship was vested in the people. Perpetual alienation could take place if and only if the provinces had given an express procuration to this affect. Even then, it was unwise, because the people were binding their posterity to take upon themselves the support of the king. Henry nearly wept with rage and cried out " They

[1] Procès Verbal des Etats de Blois, in *Recueil des pièces . . .*, vol. ii, p. 225. Bodin, *De Republica* (Frankfort, 1641), p. 523.

will not aid me with their possessions, nor will they let me use my own ".[1]

It is difficult to grasp the policy of Bodin in this assembly. He was of the moderate Catholic party; the sentiments of the cahier of Vermandois, asking for peace at present and a national council within two years, may or may not have coincided with his own opinions. He had little freedom of action. Perhaps he was not particularly interested in the religious situation except insofar as it impinged upon the political. He had a philosophic detachment on the subject of creed. On the two heads of finances and constitutional checks, he played a more active part, and seems to have exceeded his instructions. He was perfectly consistent in maintaining that fundamental laws prohibited the mortgaging of demesne lands without the consent of the nation. This was a limitation which he had explained in the Methodus, which Hotman had substantiated in *Franco-Gallia,* and upon which the publicists of the time seem to agree. He was equally right in affirming that the deputies could not vote upon this matter without further instructions from their constituencies. Since their mandates had included in many cases directions to obtain a respite from civil war, it seemed unlikely that the nation would assent to the collection by any method of funds for the prosecution of further hostilities against the Huguenots. He successfully blocked the king in his efforts to obtain any money from the people through constitutional channels.

It was in the campaign to secure legislative freedom, and in certain cases sovereignty, for the Estates, that his path seems most tortuous. Had he been won over by dining at the king's table? Was he opposing the king in an isolated

[1] Journal of Guillaume de Taix (deputy of the clergy), *Meslanges historiques* (Troyes, 1619), fol. 64 v° quoted in Henri Martin, *Histoire de France* (Paris, 1858), vol. ix, p. 460.

instance of mistaken policy, but defending monarchy by divine right as a general principle, and hence unwilling to shift the seat of sovereignty? Or had he passed through a mental crisis, and sincerely altered his point of view as to the efficacy of such a council?

The constitutional position of the Estates was uncertain. Nowhere in writing was there a clear-cut statement of their powers. The only guide was tradition, and tradition had grown befogged over the rights that they had once possessed, and those that they had tried to win. It was recognised that they had control of the purse strings for extraordinary grants, but for those only; if the king could maintain him self from the proceeds of the domain and the aides, tailles, and gabelle, then he could dispense with their counsel indefinitely. Their participation in government might therefore remain for some time in abeyance. But when they did meet, they had initiative in legislation, for they were expected to delineate the complaints of the country and to suggest measures for improvement. Having pooled their common griefs, and presented them to the king, they were dismissed. The ordinance followed some months later, drafted by the privy council in collaboration with the ruler. It was assumed that from the depths of his wisdom, the king would compose a measure correcting abuses, in the light of existing circumstances. His benevolence was taken for granted; there was no need to linger, to exercise compulsion, particularly in view of the increasing expense of a long delay. Unfortunately kings had grown neglectful and selfish; frequently the estates had been dismissed and no ordinance issued. It was time for more emphatic demands. The Estates of Pontoise had declined to discuss financial questions, until the wishes of their predecessors at Orleans had been given the form of law.[1] The Estates of Blois tried to raise

[1] *Recueil des pièces . . .*, vol. i, p. 340.

to the dignity of constitutional law their own legislative capacity.

It will be remembered that there were two distinct suggestions brought forward: (1) that a request made by any one Estate, but not accepted by both the others, should be discussed before the king by a committee composed of specially nominated judges, and twelve members of each Estate. This insured against complete neglect. (2) The second and bolder suggestions asked that any unanimous request should *ipso facto* become inviolable law. In either case the bill was to become law without submission to the approval of Parlement, whereas royal edicts must be registered by that body. The king refused the second demand, which would have subordinated him to the nation, and compromised on the first. He was willing to receive and consult with the thirty-six representatives, but would allow them no vote. (This was a perfectly obvious conclusion, for they might have constituted a majority.)

On the seventh of December, the Third Estates had eagerly sought these privileges. On the thirteenth of March they refused to accept the opportunity of conference which the king offered to them, even persuading the clergy also to refrain. This was the work of Bodin. What were his motives?

In those three months there had been altercation on religious and financial matters. The two subjects were closely bound together, and the decision anent them had cast its shadow over the third topic broached. If it had been possible to legalise unanimous demands of the Estates a long stride would have been taken toward popular rule. But since that was refused, it was extremely dangerous to place in the king's power a legitimate agent of the nation, reduced to so helpless a form. What could not be wrung from the Estates might be forced from a little group of thirty-six.

Bodin had sensed the feelings of the court with regard to uniformity in religion; what he could not check openly he had, indirectly, by preventing the collection of funds. It was impossible to foresee what measures might be suggested to the smaller group, who by intimidation might give their sanction, and bind the nation to measures similar to those just rejected. It was probably the king's financial policy which had opened his eyes; he refused a concession which would have gained more sanction for the king than voice for the Estates.

Two mysteries remain: what were the reasons which Bodin did not care to tell the archbishop of Lyons publicly, and why did he aver that the final decision was in the hands of the king, if he worked sincerely for the good of the people?

There remain, in addition to the journal of Bodin, journals by members of the clergy and of the nobility, and the procès verbal of the Third. He receives scant mention in any of these; the only document which bears him out is an account written by one Cuvelier, apparently hostile, since he calls him " Maître Jean Bodin, soi-disant deputé ", but relating that Bodin was of the opinion that the king ought to maintain peace in the realm, for they could no longer support the expense and hardships of war, and asked the observation of the Edict of Pacification.[1]

This assembly was not completely abortive. The vote on matters of religion indicated the strength of the party of compromise. It was due only to the recognition of geographical frontiers rather than numbers that the League was able to carry a majority. Paris itself, as one might expect, was the most warlike in its defense of Catholicism, but here again, there was counteraction, for the pacific views of other

[1] *Recueil des pièces . . .*, vol. ii, p. 74.

representatives of the Île de France outweighed the capital city.

On financial grounds the assembly had delivered caustic criticism of the royal regime. The Tiers commented that if the king would be more thrifty with the amounts collected, he would have enough to meet all requirements. The nobles, remembering the discovery of misappropriation of funds, requested that every penny should be employed for that purpose for which it originally was destined. All had been instructed to ask a lowering of taxes; they were unable to obtain this, but they did block the king's wishes and policies by refusing any additional grant. This was a further indication of the strength of the peace party.

They achieved no advance in legislative power. There was, however, an ordinance of 1579, which, in accordance with their expressed wished, reduced the number of officials, both judicial and administrative, and took measures to complete the codification of ordinances, as well as to reconcile the legal systems of the various provinces. This was the work which de l'Hôpital and his followers had so vehemently urged.

If the elections to these Estates were perfectly free, then the advice and information which they brought to the king was this: France preferred uniformity in religion, and hoped that the Roman Catholic faith might prevail. They were not, however, willing to go to the extreme of civil war to enforce conformity. This moderate Catholic group, as well as the Huguenots and the Leaguers, were anxious to increase the influence of the middle class in the government.

CHAPTER V

BODIN: La Republique

IN August 1576, a few months before the meeting of the Estates, Bodin had published his *République.* It was rumored that he had taken twenty years for the composition. If so, the discrepancies with the *Methodus* are even more bewildering. Twenty years would take him back to the days of the professorship in Toulouse. How then could one explain the preface:

since the sudden tempest has driven the ship of state with such violence that captain and pilots are worn out by the fray, there is need that the passengers should lend a hand. . . . Being unable to do anything better, I have undertaken this discourse on the State, in the popular tongue, for the sources of the Latin language are exhausted, and will dry up completely if the barbarity caused by the civil wars continues.[1]

He must have made a beginning sometime after March 1562, then found that he was insufficiently prepared, and put aside the work for the purpose of making a comparative study of the political growth of great nations. This resulted in the *Methodus* of 1566, published after four years of peace. He may then have returned to the large work, or perhaps his official occupations delayed his private study until after 1572. By that date there had been three civil wars, and a massacre. Shortly thereafter occurred the union of the moderate Catholics and the Huguenots under the title of Politiques, and the gathering of the retainers of the

[1] *De La République* (Paris, 1576). Introduction, no pagination.

Guises. In the course of this three-cornered quarrel, foreign armies were introduced. The age-old throne of the Capets was threatened by the diverse interests of religion, land-holding aristocracy, and rising middle class. Few rallied to its support, and Bodin, fearful of anarchy, adapted his theories to the needs of the day. He eliminated from La République his most forceful statements in favor of constitutional limitation upon the king, and made a plea for divine right monarchy, receiving its sovereignty from on high, and sharing it with no one. The end and aim of his rule was to be the establishment of God's law on earth.[1] On this one point Bodin approached the early Calvinists.

The first book of the Republic (a word which is used in its Latin sense) explains the elements of the State, its aim, and nature of the power which guides it. A State is a government of several households, and of their common interests, by a sovereign power, according to ethical laws.[2] He amplifies this declaration by a fuller discussion of the terms used; the laws which regulate family life,—marital, parental, seignorial; then the ties binding together the various households, which require definitions of such words as civis, urbs, civitas; finally an analysis of that fusion of executive, legislative and judicial powers which he places in control of all.

No definition is complete which does not indicate the purpose for which a thing exists. The most important part of Bodin's definition of a state is its aim, "according to the laws of Nature", or of God. The highest good of man, both as an individual and as a part of a group, rests upon

[1] *De La République* (Paris, 1599), p. 5.

[2] République est un droit gouvernement de plusieurs ménages, et de ce qui leur est commun, avec puissance souveraine. *De la république* (Paris, 1576), p. 1.

Respublica est familiarum rerumque inter ipsas communium, summa potestate ac ratione moderata multitudo. *De Republica* (Frankfort, 1641), p. 1.

those qualities that are peculiar to his own mind in introspection. It follows that those citizens enjoy true felicity who are informed concerning natural, human, and divine things, and who offer the fruits of their contemplations to God, the ruler of all Nature. If we grant that this is the greatest of all blessings to individuals, why shall we not allow it to be the final goal of the whole State? There are, to be sure, various types of states, with different laws and customs, built according to the ideas of different legislators. Some have stressed material advantages; fertile fields, an abundance of food, fresh water, and a mild climate. But greater than these is true wisdom, God's most splendid gift to man, from which no thief nor fire can rob him. Of course no state can exist for long that neglects those functions upon which the well-being of the citizen depends,—maintaining law, engaging in transportation of food and the many other things requisite for life. These public responsibilities although less glorious, must receive first attention. But they cannot be the final goal of any real State. God himself labored for six days; but on the seventh he rested—and that day is the more blessed.

As the state is a group of families under a certain type of government, so is family a synonym for government. It is the rule of the paterfamilias over several "subjects" and their possessions, in which we find the model for all public systems of administration. Those who preach communism in domestic life, as Plato did, would remove the strongest force for civic peace. Private property and subordination to the will of the father are essential to tranquility in the home, and stability in the state. Before man can command another, he must learn to command himself; then having acquired self-control, he may safely undertake the rule of wife, children and serfs.

When the father departs from the house in which he has

full sway, and meets with other heads of families for the common advantage, then he puts aside the name of lord and master, and assumes that of ally and citizen,—as he goes away from the family, he enters the civitas, and exchanges private affairs for public. For a citizen is only a man free in the civil sense, who is subjected to the control of another.[1] Many are the links between the different households; market place, temple, gateway, roads, laws, rights, trials, votes, customs, theaters, walls, public buildings, common fields, rewards, punishments, suits, and contracts. Before there was either civitas or Respublica, each man had power of life and death over his wife and children. But later cupidity and ferocity drove some to attack others, and when they had conquered, they enslaved their enemies. Their leader commanded, not only his own family, but also those of his allies and of his former foes; in exchange for tribute, he granted them their lives. This then was the origin of slavery and serfs, citizens and strangers, prince and tyrant.

Of various types of citizen the State is composed; native born, naturalised, or freedmen.[2] They are beneath the same sovereign rule, therefore they form a respublica, even though they differ in customs, laws, institutions, and include an infinite number of races. But if these groups use the same laws, they form not only a respublica, but a civitas, no matter how widely scattered. As there are many types of citizen, so are there variations in their powers and responsibilities. It may come about lawfully that part of the citizens is released from all offices and burdens, another part bears all.

The discussion of feudal obligation, which is one of the ties binding society (it must have been a weak link by 1576) brings Bodin to the problem of the degree of sovereignty

[1] *Cf.* the definition of p. 112, *supra.*

[2] *De Republica*, p. 75.

possessed by a feudal prince, who is the vassal of another, and thence to the problem of sovereignty as a whole. It will be remembered that this is the last abstract noun in his definition of a Republic, the very culmination of the State. Majesty, a synonym for sovereignty, is the highest power over citizens and subjects, released from the action of all law. It cannot be limited by any other power, by any laws, for any period of time. As a test, let us assume that the highest power has been granted to one man, or to several, by the people.[1] Is this the right of majesty? He decides that it cannot be, because the holder has only a precarious tenure, he is but the procurator for the people; in the end the power reverts to those who gave it. Since sovereignty by its very nature is perpetual, it cannot exist in a prince elected by the people. If on the other hand, power is granted for his lifetime, whereby the people deliberately deprive themselves, then he has sovereign rights, for there is none higher than he, but only God. Even then his edicts do not have force after his death, unless they are ratified by his successor.

No one has defined precisely what is meant by the phrase "legibus solutus". If this is taken in the sense "released from *all* law", then we shall find no prince who is really sovereign. They must all respect divine law, the laws of nature, and the common law of all nations. If they attempt to violate these, they cannot hope to escape divine wrath. The fundamental laws of the nation such as the Salic must be respected. Contracts between prince and subjects may be abrogated only with mutual consent. It is in regard to statute law alone that the Prince is free: he is permitted to nullify any laws passed by him voluntarily and without the consent of his subjects, or he may change them in part. His majesty shines forth chiefly when the estates of the people

[1] *De Republica*, p. 126.

with humble mien bring petitions to him, having no power to command, or to veto, or even to vote; the prince decides all things according to his will and judgment. Whatsoever he decrees has the force of law. Those who spread books abroad saying that the prince is bound by the will of the people, are not worthy of attention. They are merely offering a pretext to seditious men, anxious for a revolution, and rocking the ship of State. No valid reason can be produced to prove that subjects command princes, or that any power ought to be given to popular assemblies. If kings were to be held by laws of an assembly, hollow would be their power, their royal name a mockery. Under such a prince we should not have a popular state, but a gathering of a few optimates. This alone seems to be true, that whatever is made into law at the request of the people, and the command of the prince, cannot be abrogated except by the assembly.[1]

What are the rights of the sovereign? Aristotle says they are three: taking counsel, appointing magistrates, giving justice. Bodin agrees but makes a few additions, such as issuing laws without the consent of his inferiors; declaration of war and peace; dispensing power; coinage, and exaction of tribute.

Book Two deals with types of States. He lists but three, monarchy, aristocracy and democracy. Any corruption, or combination, of these, he considers as a special manifestation of one or the other type. A mixed state is an impossibility. If majesty is individual, how then at the same moment can it be the possession of one man and of all? Such a condition would mean disobedience and ultimate anarchy. Those who say that France conforms to this type, are not only in error, but are guilty of crime. It is not a crime to compare subjects to the king in regard to command

[1] *De Republica*, p. 142.

and power, to join them to him as allies? How does the democratic power manifest itself, when the Estates are assembled? Or what illustrates so well the majesty of the ruler as the humble bearing of both mighty and lowly, when with bent knee and uncovered head they revere the king? If there is no democratic element in the French government, likewise there is no aristocratic control. The court of peers is not the equal of the king, nor is the whole body of magistrates. There is of course a distinction to be made between the State, and the trend of government. The seat of sovereignty determines the type of state; it may be a monarchy, and at the same time be popularly governed, if the Prince distributes equally offices, commands and rewards, without any consideration of ability, riches, or valor; or a monarchy may be aristocratically governed, if the prince permits honors and authority to go only to the wealthy patricians.

A monarchy imposes certain limitations on its ruler, which need not apply in the case of a conquest. The victorious leader governs his new subjects without recognition of any fundamental laws, just as the paterfamilias does his serfs.

A tyrant goes further; ignoring the law of nature and of nations, he exploits their goods and liberty for his own ends. A king is one who, placed in supreme command, shows himself not less observant of the laws of nature, than he trusts his subjects, whose liberty and possessions he guards along with his own, will be, of *his* laws. This is actually the chief objective of monarchial rule; that he worship God with a pure faith, maintain the fatherland in piety, treat his neighbors with charity, the needy with benignity, deal with individual citizens impartially, govern the whole group with justice. A royal power so formed that the subjects obey the laws of the prince, and the prince the laws of nature, law reigning everywhere, so that the subjects and the prince are bound by the same chains, will create an association conducive to the happiness of all.

A tyranny, however, is a state in which one man, ignoring God's laws, treats others' goods as his own, and handles free men as though they were slaves. But it may happen that one and the same man, if he rules a vast empire, will conduct himself toward his countrymen as a king, toward those whom he has conquered in a just war as a master; but toward the remainder he will be a tyrant: or even in the same kind-dom he may act cruelly to the mighty, kindly toward the plebs. Even among tyrants, one may be worse than the other; as in virtues, so also in vices there are degrees. For what prince was ever so adorned with virtues, that he had no vices? What tyrant so abandoned, that he had no good qualities at all? They act rashly and stupidly, who pronounce sentence on a prince without knowing all his habits, circumstances, reasons,—until they have actually grasped his entire life. When we say "optimum Regem" we use popular parlance; we do not seek such a one as the heroes of old,—men of the greatest loyalty, justice, moderation, prudence, courage, and valor. They are more magnificent than true to life; such a man never existed, nor ever could exist. It is not so easy to judge a prince in whom good is tempered with evil. There are often causes, which through a combination of places, persons, or circumstances, drive him on to deeds which seem tyrannical to some, praiseworthy to others.

If a prince who has obtained the throne legitimately or otherwise, so conducts himself as to earn the reputation of a tyrant, may he lawfully be killed? That is permissible in a democracy or aristocracy, where the chief executive is appointive, but not permissible in a state where the prince is sovereign. Any one who attempts assassination, or any one who instigates another to tyrannicide, is guilty of high treason. What is to be the test of tyranny? It may be necessary to exact high taxes, yet the prince who does so is sure to be unpopular.

An aristocracy is a form of republic in which a small part of the citizens possesses the sovereignty. In this respect it offers a contrast to democracy, where the larger part of the citizens command the rest; but they are alike in this one particular, that those who have the sovereignty can indeed command the individual members, but not the group as a whole. A monarchy is superior, because one man can then command both the individuals and the group. An aristocracy is supposedly the rule of the best type of citizen, but no government was ever so constituted. It would have to come about by lot, or by the votes of the citizen, or by some combination of these methods, and virtue has nothing in common with good luck. If the people should please to express its opinion in this matter of excellence, it would not select those unlike itself, that is, the best, in an ethical sense; but it would choose those most like itself, that is, stupid, surly and swaggering, since good and wise men, if there are any, compose the smallest number of citizens everywhere. What is more shameful than that the reward of the wise should depend upon the choice of the unwise?

A democratic state is one in which all the citizens, or the greatest part thereof, have the right of commanding. Bodin feels that there never has been a popular state in which the subjects had equal rights of suffrage. The zenith of popular liberty is this: that all are on an equal plane, nor will they receive orders on any other condition than that in their turn they may command those whom they now obey. Nor even then can they be kept in control, unless the necessary and lawful measures be sweetened by largess or soft words. But since the many cannot excel in valor, riches, or noble birth, it almost always happens that the jealous multitude pursues the noble and wealthy and valorous with a certain hostility; if any one more far-seeing or public-spirited dares to restrict the excesses of the plebs who are abusing their liberty, they will not hesitate to fine him, exile, proscribe, and occasionally to condemn him to death. The more readily will they do this if he is rich, or seems to aspire to rule.

In the next book, Bodin tells of "the separate parts and members of a state, which are bound to their sovereign as though to a head,—the senate, the magistrates, curators, colleges, guilds, and orders of citizens."

The senate is a lawful gathering of those who take counsel concerning the state, and concerning those who hold the sovereignty. It is perfectly possible that a state should exist without this advisory body, for the Prince may be so wise and well-intentioned, that he will find no better counsel than his own; in special cases, he may feel such great distrust that he is unwilling to discuss affairs with any one. It is an open question, whether a government is better in the hands of an able prince ruling without an assembly, or under an incapable prince surrounded by prudent councillors. The advantage of the former method is the secrecy that it secures. Unfortunately few mortals are supremely wise, fewer princes, so that we are forced to rely upon the prudence of the assembly. Therefore the prince should be guided by the advice of the council; not only in important, but also in trifling affairs, for no greater sanction can be obtained for the decrees of prince, or people, or aristocracy, than their passage with the approval of a senate. When subjects see policies initiated without the advice, or contrary to the advice of the senate, they despise them, count them for naught, or obey only halfheartedly the commands of emperor or magistrate; moreover the seditious voices of the people are raised, and conspiracies are formed against the leader.

Since the Senate is as necessary in a Republic as mind and reason in the body, it should meet regularly at stated place and time. Only the elders are admissible; their accumulated experience is of value to the state. Bodin excludes the senile and the corrupt, although he offers no better test of integrity than acceptance by the whole Senate. The total number must be small, for not many men are sufficiently endowed; furthermore too large a number eliminates the possibility of secrecy. Popular states are often forced to appoint a large number of senators, in order to conciliate ambitious men. To counterbalance the publicity of this, there should be a smaller and more private assembly for matters which it would be dangerous to spread abroad. Hardly a contemporary state existed which did not have a privy council in addition to its senate.

Senators should have the right of initiation of business. It is not just that the prince alone should introduce material for discussion; this is a perilous procedure, for so much authority is given to one man, in stating his opinion first that the others do not dare to express themselves. Stress is laid upon the purely advisory capacity of the Senate, as distinct from any sovereign capacity. If we inquire whether supremacy ought to be given to this body, we must answer in the negative; such powers could not be granted without diminution of majesty. On one occasion the king's sovereignty chiefly shines forth,—when he weighs the opinion of the Senate, but is not forced to abide by a majority decision. If it seems to any one absurd that the magistrates and courts give commands, but not the Senate, although it has power to settle differences between these lesser bodies, one ought to remember, that magistrates have authority only in certain specified fields, to execute the laws of the realm. The decrees of the Senate have no force, unless the Prince (or whatever group has the sovereignty) gives to them validity. So, in a monarchy the name and sanction of the prince must be affixed to the acts of the Senate. If it is asked, why this should be, the chief reason in this: the Senate would be at one and the same time the adviser and the sovereign; it would have to decide upon the best policies, and likewise execute them, and in that case there would be no authority of people, peers, or king: all things would depend upon the caprice of the Senate alone. Those who would give the Senate sovereignty are attempting the ruin of the Republic.

In olden times the court of Parlement was the Senate of the realm of France, but since it was occupied with settling lawsuits, and could not easily move from the city, the king founded the great council. This in its turn became specialized in legal affairs and Francis I deprived it of all share in political administration, while he set up another and smaller body, the privy council. As this grew unwieldly in size through favoritism, still another and more private body took its place. Speed and secrecy were the motives.

Although in public law many things are illuminating and fruitful, yet perhaps the most fruitful is discussion about public officials; and although many things have been published about magistrates and the subject is well worn, yet it lies veiled in obscurity, because the people who wrote about it never defined anything clearly. Bodin therefore starts with a definition. An official is a public person who has a duty defined by law. A curator is one who fulfills a special duty beyond the law, by the will of the ruler. A magistrate is one who has public authority. This authority lasts only so long as it shall seem good to the prince, and its precarious nature eliminates all pretension to absolute power. The prince has the right to appoint magistrates, whom he selects according to the prudence and virtues of each candidate; usually from the nobles or the wealthy. Since these appointees have very great powers and important duties committed to their charge, it is necessary to distinguish exactly what is due from the magistrate to the sovereign. The Prince differs from the magistrate in this respect, that he sees no one in the Republic to compare with him or to precede him: placed in the rank next below the lofty and immortal God, he looks down upon the citizens at a great distance from him. He gives to the magistrate certain power over the lives of private citizens and others which pertain to the State itself. For the immediate purpose of writing, Bodin considers only the latter important, and feels that their exercise gives rise to two fundamental questions: ought the magistrate to obey a prince who commands unjust things? Or if not, should he go so far as to offer resistance to his sovereign? Those commands which are in keeping with divine and natural laws, he should obey, and even those in conflict with the laws of other nations. If the prince ordains anything contrary to the laws and customs of the realm which he swore to maintain, the magistrates must still follow, since his office does not permit him to estimate the justice of imperial commands. But if he is ordered to put aside a former law which has been superseded by more recent legislation, he must sustain the old law while he admonishes the prince, not once, but several times. The magistrate should abdicate rather than swear to laws which he feels are iniquitous, although others may approve. Often the wisest man is in a minority, resisting a foolish multitude; but when the prince himself definitely commands, the magistrate should warn him, and reveal the difficulties. Then he must obey, otherwise the majesty of the state would depend upon the will of the magistrate, giving a bad example to the people. If they should begin to despise the commands of the prince, the ruin of the state would come about.

So far as the relations between the magistrate and the people are concerned, he has power to command and to prohibit; he may apply force. He is the living and breathing force of the law. From this, it ought to be clear that there are two kinds of public command: one, the highest, absolute, infinite, above the laws and the orders of the magistrate; the other, lawful, subject to the sovereign, peculiar to those who have power to command until permission is withdrawn or the term expires. The sovereign has no mortal peer; whereas the magistrate receives his share of authority from the sovereign, and must obey him. The private citizen, after immortal God, is bound by the laws of majesty, and the order of the magistrate.

All states and empires are held in check by law, equity, the action of the law, and the office of the magistrate. The law is related to the action of the law, just as equity is, to the office of the magistrate. Likewise a decision is rendered according to law, but a decree according to equity. Whatever a judge decides according to equity and his own ideas, is called a decretum; but when he decides according to the prescript of the sovereign, this really is a judicium.

Other important groups within the State are the colleges, corps, and the universitas; these Bodin defines as follows: a college is a lawful association of three or more persons of the same condition; a corps is the union of several colleges; the universitas is the multitude of all the families, colleges and corps in the same city, united under a common bond of law. Men have always sought the society of others, going gradually from the natural group of the family to the college, corps, universitas, and finally to the civitas, and to the empires which have been set up. These associations are founded first upon love, then upon mutual affection and justice which could not exist otherwise than through them. Whoever thinks that the Republic could dispense with brotherhoods, would seem to imply that it can subsist without love and friendship, but under such conditions not even the world could maintain its course. The royal power, modified by the wisest laws and institutes, can have no firmer or more stable surety than corps and colleges. If the king has need of resources, money, or an army, he can obtain them more easily through the assistance of these groups. Moreover those very people who urge the destruction of the assembly which the Spanish call curia, the English, Parliament, are the very ones who in pressing danger, flee to these assemblies as to a sacred asylum, in order to protect themselves and the State from the enemy. What better place of discussion for the ills of the State, assistance to the people, change of regulations, than before the prince, in the Senate, before the people? There are explained the complaints of the lowly, the injuries of the great, theft and larceny, that would otherwise have been unknown to the prince. There are heard the pleas of each order. It is unbelievable with what joy the people [plebs] see the prince meeting the assembly! How well-content they are to listen to him speaking! How each one strives to be seen by him!

For this reason the English and Spanish have wisely ordained that a meeting of the popular assembly should take place every third year; in order that the prince may do this more willingly, they grant no tribute to him, until the convention is held. The French kings do not summon the general estates so often as the English, but there are six provinces which have their own local gatherings. How necessary these popular assemblies are, may be understood from the fact that those people who have the right of expression are the more tractable; others have to be forced; the voices of individual citizens are indistinguishable, but the voice of a whole province is very clear, and its plea so efficacious that the prince cannot spurn it, even if he would. The services of these councils are innumerable. If it is a question of recruiting an army, collecting taxes, raising money to repel an enemy or to punish bandits, to build ports, citadels, walls, to execute repairs, and matters of this sort, which cannot possibly be accomplished by individual effort—their united energy will produce a successful conclusion.

In the Latin edition there is an additional chapter at the end of Book III, entitled *De ordinibus civium,* in which Bodin expresses surprisingly democratic views regarding the social value of the small merchant class, and the inglorious career of the luxuriously idle.

The topics of Book IV are the origin, growth, and type of the State; the change from one type to another; the decline and fall.

All states take their origin from the family, or in certain special cases, from colonisation by another state. No matter what the fundamental elements, the actual government was set up either by force, or by voluntary submission to one man. A popular or aristocratic state is more difficult to found and to maintain. Hereditary monarchies, on the other hand, rarely alter, since a king, even though evil, shines in the reflected glory of his virtuous father. But changes in an empire may dawn rather swiftly if the ruler is a prey to vices; lust has ruined more states than cruelty, for men are terrified by cruelty, but the passions of a tyrant stir the subjects not only to anger, but also to contempt. They consider him unworthy to command them, since he cannot command himself. Those kingdoms which have to be held together by fear and force, will not long endure.

A lengthy chapter explains the influence of the stars on the fortunes of states, and attempts a refutation of certain phases of the Copernican theory. The contradictory mentality of Bodin, with its modern critical tendencies founded on a substratum of medieval love of authority, is nowhere more apparent than here, when he turns aside from the discussion of deliberative assemblies, to note the marvellous properties of numbers.

The first law of a well ordered Republic is the maintenance of the characteristics of that particular type of government, and especially the prevention of any threatening conditions. Antiquity is so dear to everyone that an ancient law can easily hold respect without magistrates, but a new law can hardly exist without hope of reward, fear of punishment, or the assistance of officials. From this fact it follows that the utility of a new law is not so great as its inconveniences. It is important to bear this in mind, for peril threatens, if an attempt is made to alter the fundamental laws of the state. They ought to be immutable, not because the state must serve the laws, but rather that the laws serve the state and society. Nothing should be done suddenly and violently but gradually, as a physician cures the sick. How then are we to diminish the authority of a living prince, or take it away altogether? It is dangerous for the state, as well as for the prince himself, to take away all power from all the magistrates at one and the same moment. One of the best securities in France is the fact that when the king dies, the magistrates continue in office to protect the state. Let us imitate Almighty God, who moves slowly in His appointed way. He plants little seeds to grow into lofty trees silently that no one may know. So does He fit together extremes and contraries with such wisdom that no violence is done.

No cause of revolution is more frequent than rivalry over appointment to office. Hence it would seem pertinent to consider whether magistrates should be appointed for a year or for life. The chief argument in favor of a brief term is this: for all public affairs the main objective is virtue. The activities of the magistrate should aim to produce excellent citizens. There is no better way of obtaining this result than to distribute rewards for worthy conduct, and no prize is more effective than that very honor of holding office, which it is unseemly to measure by utility or gain. Virtue has no greater enemy than a mercenary utilitarianism, if indeed in its essence, utility can be separated from virtue, to which it clings by its very nature. A wise ruler will therefore reward all his subjects with honors and office, each in accordance with his deserts. This could not be done, if the term were for life. For the purpose of destroying all excuse for sedition, nothing is so important as equality in treatment, and an equal distribution of responsibility and rewards. It is unwise to confine the possibilities of office to a limited circle, yet that obviously results, if magistrates are to be perpetual. He who has attained a permanent office is liable to spend his time in the enjoyment of his own virtue. Who would check the wicked from a life of crime, unless they were restrained by fear of punishment? Who would make charges against perpetual magistrates whom no one can touch?

On the other hand, valuable experience is not put to use by this method of frequent rotation. After all, public utility should be the supreme guide, not the satisfaction of petty ambitions. There can be no continuity of policy without a long term, nor can a magistrate exercise independent judgment, when he knows that as a private citizen, he may later incur the malice of those whom he has convicted. Michel de l'Hôpital thought that all authority ought to be assigned for a limited period. But he forgot, and indeed it has never been sufficiently emphasised, that the customs of a state must vary according to its aim. Those laws which nourish popular liberty, would overturn a monarchy: in this group falls the frequent change of magistrates. In a monarchy, in which there is a unique sovereign, subjects should have no ambition to command, but rather the habit of obedience. The king should alter the length of the term of office according to his best judgment in each individual case. By this system, the officers will not all be changed at the same moment, so that the Republic will not be without assistants, furthermore the incapable will never be called to take their turn in holding office.

Princes originally were created for the sake of justice. When the Hebrews appointed Samuel to be their king they imposed this obligation on the prince toward his subjects, an obligation which was indeed mutual, " ut non magis principi parere subditi debeant, quam princeps subditis jus dicere ". However, it is no longer expedient for kings to undertake this function; frequently in contemporary history, they are vicious; even if they are worthy, they should permit agents to punish. It is for the prince to win the love of his subjects by clemency. Let magistrates condemn. It was a wise policy of former days, when they constituted La Chambre Criminelle des Parlements, to change the membership every three months, so that the habit of pronouncing capital punishment might not harden the natural kindliness of the judges. There is nothing which can so weaken a state as to despoil the Senate or the magistrates of their ordinary lawful functions, and to hand over everything to the sovereign, for the less the power of the sovereign (reserving the true marks of majesty), the more stable it is. The State cannot fail to prosper when the prince exercises those rights which pertain to majesty, the Senate keeps its authority, the magistrates exercise their power and justice follows its ordinary course; they are very much mistaken who think to augment the power of the prince by pointing out his prerogatives and implying that his wish, his nod, his expression are an edict in themselves, a decree, a law, so that no subject can perform an official act which cannot be nullified by him.

Civil warfare is particularly dangerous for popular and aristocratic states, for there is no one who can check the group, unless a majority can force the rebels to obey. Freedom of speech is perilous. The eloquence of wicked citizens is more to be feared than the pest, than the sword of a madman; but nothing is more admirable if a good man uses eloquence for the protection of the innocent, the terror of the wicked, an ornament for the worthy. There is nothing which can coerce the seditious, or restrain the attacks of furious people, or recall them to their right minds more readily than eloquence. This applies to a popular state more than to any other.

Book V is introduced by a chapter repeating the climatic theory which Bodin had published in the Methodus. He attempts to explain what laws are suited to any given people and what form of government; from what causes are determined the customs and nature of races. The differences in appearance and character of men vary according to their habitat, for in the same climate of East or West, a slight gradation makes a great change in the natives. Even in the Mediterranean area those who live in the north differ in physique and intellectual traits from those who dwell in the Southeast. Moreover among those who seek a home not only in this same Mediterranean area, but even in the same region, equally remote from the equator, under the same heavens, almost in the same spot, there are vast differences between the mountaineers and the valley-dwellers. The Oriental is by nature softer than the Westerner, more talkative, vivacious, gregarious. The Northerner surpasses the Easterner in strength, size, form and color, but he is eclipsed by the Easterner in cleverness. The migration of peoples however, have produced alterations of mind and body in all races.

In the wintertime we observe that caves and wells are warm, and the animals exhale warm air, but in the summer the caverns of the earth are cold. A similar condition exists among human beings; those who live in the North, burn within, but the south-easterners are cold. Those who have more heat can digest more easily, which explains why the Northerners are larger, and eat more animal food. The inhabitants of the intervening regions, which on account of the moderation of heat and cold are suitable for a happier and more healthful life, are endowed with somewhat mediocre strength of body and only normal shrewdness. Therein is seen the wisdom of God, which separates sagacity and greatness of spirit from strength of body, since He recognised that nothing was more cruel than injustice equipped with strong armies. So the peoples who live in the middle regions have more spirit and sagacity, but less strength, than those of the South-east, by whom they are exceeded in sagacity, but not in spirit and courage. Then too they have more skill in command, and are more just in managing affairs than either of the other groups.

Bodin observed in the writings of ancient times that armies came from the North, but the abstruse sciences, philosophy, mathematics, religion, and systems of true investigation came from the Southeast; the art of governing and directing the state, and the science of laws, took their beginnings in the midportions.

We can therefore judge what type of state suits each place. The mountaineers love liberty, and the whole northern group favors popular government or free (liberas) monarchies, for they agree to give the command to prudent princes, and to take it away as often as they desire. Strength and vitality make the mountaineer impatient of tyranny and of obedience, and so among the Helvetians we find popular government. Those who think to change this state into a monarchy delude themselves; although a monarchy is superior to popular rule, yet it is advisable first to learn what each nation desires. The mountain peoples must learn the gentler arts, before they can be content with a kingdom. It is odd that windswept areas produce fierce and restless men, but quiet places have a more contented and civilised population. No one can have a tranquil mind who is constantly tossed about. No one can meditate who is in action, but only those with a mind clear of all perturbation, and a motionless body.

A group of people upon whom an inappropriate system of laws has been imposed, soon reverts to type. If colonies are led to far distant regions they will not change in character so soon as their children, who draw their substance from the new lands; in a short while the second generation will differ from the older stock. We see the change in the Goths, who once upon a time conquered Spain and Toulouse, and the alteration in the Frankish colonists who were settled in Germany. The French have been unfairly accused of levity by ancient writers. Really their outstanding characteristic is their religious ardor, in which for six hundred years they have shown the utmost constancy.

Bodin's moral philosophy is well summarised at the end of this chapter.

In words and deeds of men, as in all things, I have always held that golden mean, which is called constantia, and which steers a middle course between stubbornness and levity: many divide persistency from stubbornness and call one a virtue, the other a vice. However that may be, I suppose that wise men never have approved a perpetual stand in any one opinion, but as in navigation it is an art to run before the tempest, even if one cannot make port, so in human affairs, which are varied and dissimilar, I think it is possible to change an opinion honorably. Those who defend their own opinions stubbornly think it base to be put in the wrong, and wicked to be conquered. They prefer to give up their life, rather than their opinions. Such people are of no use to themselves, or to the state.[1]

Although there are many things which may lead to a change of government, or the ruin of a state, nothing is more

[1] *De Republica* (Frankfort, 1641), Book V, Chapter I.

potent than the riches of the few and the unendurable poverty of the many. A multitude of idle men, wandering hither and thither, seizing the goods of private citizens, place all their hopes of fortune in overthrowing the State. This was the reason why ancient legislators, such as Lycurgus and Plato, advocated an equal division of the fields. Bodin does not approve this course, which would violate justice, and tend to the destruction of the state. He opposes also any restriction in the birth rate, since population affords strength to the government, but hints that the church holds more land than is fitting for the good of the state. The clergy constitute a hundredth part of the people, yet they own a tenth of the flocks and crops, of which they have obtained a large part by compulsion. He even refers to the attempts of Edward I to prevent too great an accumulation of territory in mortmain.

It is the task of a prudent prince to distribute honors and rewards moderately or even sparingly, and only to those who have merited well of the state. The greatest misfortune that can afflict a government is the sale of offices, which should have gone as a reward to capable and self-sacrificing citizens. All nations have sought by wise laws to prevent this custom; the ordinances of St. Louis forbidding favoritism in appointments to the judicature were observed until the time of Francis I. Those who auction off posts in the government, sell the most sacred thing in the world, justice; they also sell the state, and the blood of its subjects; they sell the law, and in removing from the courts honor, virtue, knowledge, piety, they throw wide open the doors to theft, conspiracy, avarice, ignorance and impiety. The poverty of the prince is no excuse. Every one knows how the proceeds of the kingdom have been distributed to unworthy favorites, thereby undermining the fairest realm in Europe. In 1572, gifts were made to the extent of 2,700,000 livres; in 1573,

2,044,000 livres; in 1574, 547,000 livres;[1] in the six months following, 955,000 livres; these figures did not include pensions, which could not have been less than 200,000 livres. Most of the money came from the sale of office to the highest bidder.

Book VI reviews the material already covered: origins, progress, growth, type, change, rights of the sovereign, body of magistrates, orders of citizens, by what arts the group of citizens live together, and the laws of compacts. There remain for discussion, common fields, the treasury, taxes, jurisdiction, the very things upon which the community of citizens rests and is supported.

The censorship was created originally for the evaluation of private possessions, but there are many other uses. One can easily obtain the age, order, condition of citizens, their number, how many capable of bearing arms, how many should be sent forth to colonies, how many trained in public works, and how large a food supply is necessary for the state. The census is useful also for the purpose of equalising taxation, for through information obtained in this way we can learn of the wants and the just complaints of the weak, and particularly of the agricultural classes, who struggle under such a weight of taxes and tribute that they must often abandon their fields and their homes. From these same tables we could learn who is poor, who is wealthy, who spendthrift, who avaricious, what resources are needed for each trade. In cases where a judge had to impose a pecuniary penalty, he could apportion the amount to the resources of the defendant. Bodin would maintain a strict censorship over plays, because of their influence on the manners and morals of youth. This should not be placed in the hands of the clergy, for in their attempts to extend their jurisdiction and empire, they might lose not only legal, but also moral,

[1] *De la république* (Paris, 1576), p. 577.

command. To be sure, the causes of religion and of morals go hand in hand, and he would prefer that both should be handed over to the clergy, if they had representatives of the priesthood who were such as they ought to be, that is, excelling all others in the highest integrity, faith, loyalty, piety, wisdom, and knowledge of administration.

Discussion of finances is confined to three heads (1) honorable means of filling the treasury; (2) useful expenditure of public money; (3) check on lavish distribution.

Funds may properly be obtained from the public lands, from the spoils of the enemy, from gifts, from allied tribute, from commerce conducted by the state, from imports and exports, and from personal taxes. Public lands have been set apart exactly for this purpose. In a monarchy, the domain lands are intended for the personal maintenance of the king, and the fisc for general expenses, such as salaries. But they belong to the state, not to the king, and cannot be alienated without the consent of Parlement. That good king of France who was called the father of his people, was unwilling to mix public resources with private, and so created a separate management for his lands of Blois and Montfort, which illustrates well the fact that the two funds are distinct. It is not permissible for a sovereign prince to take over all the revenues in time of peace, since he has only the usufruct, and must reserve the surplus for public necessities. There results a sharp distinction between the conduct of the treasury in a monarchial state, and that in a popular or in an aristocratic state, where nothing which belongs to the state can be applied to private uses. In fact public property is usually abused in a popular regime, for the magistrates take over every thing they can lay hands upon for their own uses; each one tries to please his friends, or to gratify the people at the expense of the state.

It should not be necessary to tax the citizens until all

other resources have proved insufficient. In a crisis it is the pious duty of the citizens to give their money to save the state. This kind of tax was called extraordinary, but is becoming ordinary; there is a third kind, the casual. It was ordained at the Estates of 1338, in the presence of king Philip VI, that no tax should be levied on the people without its sanction, a system which has been maintained in Spain, England, and Germany. Commines supported the same principle in 1484. The Helvetians differ from the French in the incidence of taxation, for they command tribute from the nobles and the wealthy, and spare the poor. But in France we see the lords spiritual and the nobility, rich in worldly goods, suffer the wretched plowmen and artisans to struggle under the burden of all sorts of tribute. Not only this, but certain powerful boroughs have been excused. Thus it has come about that the wealthy towns, the nobility, and the ecclesiastical order have left the whole burden to the lowest class, who are crushed beneath the load. The Church is forced to contribute tenths, and irregular gifts; the nobles to sell their property to go to war at their own expense. The ancients had a wiser arrangement; the taxes fell upon real property. Languedoc and Provence have followed this system, so that the rich and poor, the noble, the common folk, the priest and the laborer are on an equal footing. Bodin suggests as the fairest type of tax, one on luxuries—gold and silver, perfume, cosmetics, jewels, and objects of this description, which ought not to be prohibited,—which indeed cannot be, for such is the nature of man that he seeks nothing more eagerly than that most solemnly forbidden. Wherefore the northern princes obtain large returns from the tax on wine, with which their subjects could very well dispense, but are unwilling. A change in apportionment is desirable, but a reduction in the total is impracticable. Those who urge that the taxes should be reduced to the amount collected in the time of Louis XII do not recognise that since that period gold and silver have been pouring in from newly discovered lands, particularly from Peru, so that the cost of everything is ten times greater than it used to be.

The state should use its collected riches for the public dignity and safety. Our forefathers were accustomed to distribute first among the needy a share of the funds requested by the king; the next apportionment was for the palace of the king; the third for repairs. But now the order is reversed. Yet no government flourishes so well as those which care for the needy and ailing. At present it is considered best to give the first attention to the prince and his family, then to the soldiers' pay, then to the magistrates, then to those who have earned a reward from the state, finally to the lowly subjects, not because of that common humanity which links us with them, but because the state might be disturbed by the distress of the lower classes. After these matters have been settled, the fortresses must be strengthened, the walls restored, bridges erected, roads repaired, ports built, ships constructed, temples raised, public buildings renovated, and new ones added.

It was wisely ordained in 1542 that each year the financial officer of each generality should send to the treasury two statements, one containing the estimated revenue for the coming year, the other the actual receipts of the preceding year. The treasurer should then make two summaries of the financial condition for the entire kingdom, so that the king and his council may know at a glance the state of the finances, and thereby regulate gifts, benevolence and expense. Unfortunately the king rarely sees such a statement. Without going any further back than 1572, we find that an estimate was made of 2,000,000 livres tournois for sundry expenses. Actually, at the end of the year 8,200,000 livres had been spent for this item; if the king had known the condition of the treasury or if he had kept a record of the amount of his gifts, the names of the recipients, and the cause of the donation, matters could not have reached such a pass.

To any one considering the bases of the state the matter of coinage seems not only important, but even vital to the community. Depreciation of the currency cannot take place without loss to onc and all. But not only is it impossible to lower the money without disadvantage to the state; it cannot even be altered, since the change of value and material of the coins casts a doubt on the census and the possessions of each man. Whence it comes about that no one feels safe, no matter how wealthy he may be. Uncertainty is thrown upon the contracts which have been made in associations, in wardships, trusts, mandates, goods bought and sold, the very ties which unite society: revenue is uncertain, taxes, tribute, the prizes and penalties which are imposed by law; finally the resources of the treasury, and many things both in public and private affairs must necessarily become unreliable. It can therefore be understood what great danger threatens the state if the prince arbitrarily depreciates the coins. An oath is an insufficient safeguard; the value and weight of money should be fixed by means so secure that neither prince nor subject can alter it, even if he wished.

A popular state seems praiseworthy to many, because it extends to all equal rights. Nature makes no distinction between one man and another, so far as honors and riches are concerned, and the democracy keeps this same end in view. But these arguments are no stronger than spiders' webs, for there never was a state able to maintain that complete equality of honor, opportunity and power for all. Nature itself does not achieve it. Who has not observed that there are beings so superior that we must inevitably obey them? And how many men are stupid and surly, with no native ability or talent? If liberty exists in a democracy, as they so loudly boast, certainly there is not much freedom left by the laws and the magistrates. Never did a monarchy, or an aristocracy have so many officials as we see in a democracy. Furthermore the corruption in public affairs is very great. The power is really in the hands of the magistrates, and if they disagree, there is a crisis in the government. What can be more absurd than to regard as law the reckless wishes of a fickle and unskilled multitude, which grants honors more often by a blind impulse than by a weighted judgment? What more mad, than to seek counsel from the plebs when the state is in danger? The final goal of the state is the maintenance of piety, justice, fortitude, and especially prudence, but the popular state places such emphasis upon competition that all higher motives are crushed. Upright men are in a minority, but the wicked are multitudinous, and throng forward to obtain command. Those who think to establish equality of honor and command in the state, wish to give over the helm to these unskilled, reckless, half foolish people, as well as to the wise. They count the votes, instead of weighing them. Since the family is the model for the State, let the defenders of popular government try it in their own homes. Governments of this type are constantly in dissension. One might perhaps argue that the Helvetian state has prospered long and peacefully, but this is a very special case. In the first place, the mountainous nature of the country has affected the character of the people; then too they have made a practice of sending forth their unruly citizens to fight as mercenaries, so that while they seem to be governed in popular fashion, they are really aristocracies.

The arguments of those who defend aristocracy are more difficult to answer. The best type of aristocracy is that in which the optimates are selected for their virtue; as one dies, another is chosen by suffrage. Thus it comes about that no one is denied access to honor and command, except those who are unworthy. But even in this small group some one man must be superior to all the others, and so his guidance would be best for the state. Of course it is a disadvantage that there must occur a change of leader, at the death of the prince,—an alteration in policy is unfortunate. If, however, the succession is established by law, this difficulty will to some extent be obviated. No women, and no descendants through women are permitted to ascend the throne, but only the eldest male, of the line of the eldest male.

Secrecy in counsel, rapidity in decision, efficiency in execution, follow from the supremacy of one man. Legislators, historians, philosophers and theologians with one voice are agreed that the kingdom is the finest type of government, that which contributes most to the happiness of the people. But the sovereignty can not be shared with any gathering of optimates or people without danger to the state; the supreme power might dissolve in anarchy, or uprisings of the lower classes might occur. This should be borne in mind lest we pay too much heed to the voices of the untrained, who think that the prince should be subordinated to a popular assembly, and from them receive laws. The prince should of course listen to the varying opinions of the senators; but it is better for him to select that decision which appears best to him, than to permit the conflicting senators to attempt a choice. If the state is really unique, a single entity, how can it have more than one head? Is not this the pattern set by nature?

This vast treatise of seven hundred odd folio pages, is not confined to political theory. The author deals also with economics and the more practical problems of government. He has some knowledge of science, although so tinctured with astrology and alchemy that he draws erroneous conclusions from the data ferreted out by his inquisitive mind. A philosophy of compromise pervades the whole. It is not easily read, for the very richness of his material has embarassed the author into a diffusiveness which obscures the issue. The digressions, in so far as they depict events then current, or portray the mental outlook of a sixteenth century savant, cannot fail to interest, but there is undoubtedly confusion in the thought, and occasionally contradiction. Sometimes this contradiction is only apparent, being caused by want of an exact terminology; for instance the same word "loi" has to be applied to various different types of commandment. At other times Bodin plainly contradicts himself, as when he says in Book I Chapter IX that coining money is one of the rights of sovereignty, but in Book VI Chapter III that the weight of coins should be established by a law so binding that no prince would dare to depreciate the currency.

He apparently had been cogitating over half a dozen related problems: What is a State, and what are its constituent elements? What are the various types of statehood? By what means does the most general type of state function? What has been the moral development of the generalised state? Why are there variations among states, and within a state? What is the best method of administering a state? Having reached conclusions satisfactory to himself, he did not trouble to eliminate, if indeed he noticed, some minor inconsistencies. The supremacy of the sovereign, which he upholds in Book I, is impossible to maintain in Book VI, when he deals with the practical details of administration.

To summarise: a state is a form of government, composed of various units of a more elementary type of government, the family. This becomes the model for the machinery of the State, the subjects having the same relation to the sovereign as the members of the family to the father. The authority of the sovereign in the State, however, is not quite so powerful as the parental control in the family. To be sure, the prince has no peer and no superior, but the Deity; yet he is bound to respect not only Divine law and the laws of nature, which limit the paterfamilias also, but the common law of nations, the fundamental laws of his own particular kingdom, and such ordinances as have been issued by him at the request of the people. In applying to him the term *legibus solutus,* we must recognise that it is only his own arbitrarily issued edicts from whose action he is released, and those of his predecessors, similarly issued, which are no longer of benefit to the kingdom.[1]

Since the basis of family rule is the superior strength of the father, analogy forces Bodin to the conclusion that the State originated in conquest. This accounts for the complete subordination of all advisory bodies, such as assembly or magistrates. Although it is recognised that there are other manifestations of sovereignty than that vested in one man, yet by constantly reverting to that form, he implies his preference for a monarchy. All states, whether democratic, aristocratic, or royal, owe their foundation and continuation to God's will, and if properly constituted, deem the establishment of His law their chief concern.

Any attempt to divide the sovereignty among the factions representative of people, intellectuals, and leader is doomed to failure, owing to the very nature of sovereignty. A pluralist state is to Bodin unthinkable. He rejects it for France in particular, and in general for any state which has ever existed. He disproves also the possibility of an aristocracy or democracy, in the pure sense of either term, and declares his preference for the rule of one man. In this phase he rec-

[1] But *cf.* material on magistrates, in Ch. III, Book I.

ognises three types, varying according to the king of limitation which the monarch takes upon himself, and degenerating into the tyrant who knows no restriction. It is characteristic of his divine-right tendencies that he permits the assassination of a tyrannical executive who holds delegated authority, but not an attack upon the king's majesty. There is an implicit theory that subjects are not capable even of estimating the king's conduct.

An ideal state would be one in which the prince was all-wise, and had no need of earthly advice. Bodin complicates his divine right theories by admitting that few princes are of such a character, and although they stand in the rank next to God, at an immense distance from their subjects, he suggests that the ship of state will ride more steadily if some of these lowly beings are summoned for counsel. This is intended not only to supplement the wisdom of the prince, but also to supply him with information and the nation with an opportunity for expression and cooperation.

In his enthusiastic advocacy of groups within the Republic, one might almost fancy that Bodin were deviating from his monist State. But there is no question of divided allegiance; while he realises the advantages and necessity to themselves and the government, of associations of all sorts, he grants to them deliberative functions only. Loyalty to the group, as opposed to loyalty to the sovereign, or even a moment's hesitation between the two, is impossible. The magistrate who realises that his chief has made an error, must resign, rather than question the power from which his own small share of authority derives its source. This conclusion is due not so much to respect for a divinely inspired sovereign, as to the practical motive of preventing riots in the State. Authority must be unique and unquestioned.

Book IV seems less absolute in its trend than the earlier parts of the work. While the fundamental cause for the creation of government was force,—either a successful conquest, of concerted action against a possible conquest—this cannot be the only element in maintaining control. Efficiency and integrity are equally necessary. It is interesting to find that Bodin mentions two different types of original compact. The unilateral, voluntary submission of a group to one leader, through motives of defense, and the bilateral, when Samuel is required to give justice in return for obedience. While he avoids any suggestion of action in case of a violated contract, nevertheless he deprecates undue extension of the authority of the sovereign, if this is to entail the weakening of the advisory bodies.

There is an echo of contemporary conditions in the chapter on civil strife, and the attitude of the executive thereto. Bodin advocates here the same course which he was later to uphold at Blois—reasonable discussion, and an attempt to allay the violence of the ignorant by swaying their emotions, rather than by the sword.

He himself declares that his first four books deal with the general problem, whereas the last two apply to particular instances and operations of government. He has observed inequalities in the distribution of wealth that seem to threaten the stability of the state, but prefers to alleviate this condition by public benevolence, rather than by nationalisation of the land. Appeal to ambition and glory is a potent argument for winning loyalty and support to the state, but honors and office must be bestowed with the greatest care. The system of venality, which was to load France with superfluous officials for two more centuries seems to him to strike at the foundations of the state. In addition to the effect of climate upon character, Montesquieu appears to have taken over this theory of honor as the basic principle in a monarchy.

In accordance with his absolutist tendencies Bodin yields

to the government a high degree of initiative in prying out the private affairs, and in regulating the lives, of its subjects. To be sure, this information is to be used for a good purpose, as ever with him; there is to be a sliding scale for taxation and penalties; young people must be protected from vice.

His opinions on finance, far from strengthening the powers of the monarch, seem rather to restrict his sovereignty. Under ordinary circumstances, the king of France is expected to subsist on the revenue from lands set apart especially for that purpose, but this property is not his own. He has the use of it for his lifetime, but he cannot sell it or mortgage it, without the consent of the representatives of the real owner, the nation. If a crisis occasions the need for additional funds, again the nation must be consulted, for private property cannot be appropriated without sanction.

Modern nationalism has applied his suggested tax on consumption only to imports, lest native production should dwindle, with resulting unemployment. Yet Bodin by this very means had hoped to lighten the burden of the laboring class, and to force the luxurious to pay their share of the expenses of government. On this score, as elsewhere, he shows a realisation of glaring inequalities which led to later revolution. His balance sheets sounds like a forecast of Necker's Compte Rendu. His copious dissertation on the difficulties of bimetalism, and its bearing on the currency problem, was probably based on statistical information during the meeting of the Estates General. At the end of Chapter III, Book VI of *The Republic,* he says "When I went as delegate to the Estates at Blois, I was commanded by the prince to confer with financial officers concerning the coinage, which was causing concern. There we discussed briefly the rumors abroad."

Towards society as a whole he maintains an intellectual

aloofness. He obviously despises the rabble, yet admits their common humanity, and makes some attempt to ameliorate their lot, though he would grant no political rights. No definite preference in religion is indicated, but for the sake of stability in the state, he urges uniformity, and presumably, though not specifically adherence to the Church of Rome. He ventures however to make a veiled criticism on the moral integrity of the clergy, and a more pointed attack on their vast landed interests,—here again noting an ultimate cause of cataclysm.

In the ten years since the publication of the *Methodus,* his concept of the kingship had perceptibly altered. The king of France in 1566, as in 1576, had stood as intermediator between God and his people. But in the earlier period there had been some recognition of the nation, or delegates of the nation, as assistant in the business of governing—a source of information, advice, and prohibition. By 1576 the prohibitory function had become inhibited, in Bodin's thought. The king was above all but God. From an immense distance he looked down upon his subjects. In this situation he would have to recognise Divine law; strangely enough, although they had no bearing upon his supernatural position, he was bound also by the fundamental laws of the land. This may have been due to the fact that prescription meant recognition, or at all events, toleration, by generations of divinely inspired monarchs, so that the king must comply, in respect to his ancestors. This excuse would not hold, however, for another check upon his will,—he must obey those decrees which he has made conjointly with the national assembly. So far as the raising of tribute is concerned, his hands again are tied by prescription.

But the source of law is the king. His office was originally protective and judicial (in some cases despotic, but ultimately judicial); before he made statute law, he decided cases, thereby developing customary law. In more recent days, he has laid aside the actual fulfillment of the judicial function, but he still makes law,—statute law, now—and what he himself has made, he may alter or antequate, or openly annul. He is free from the constraint of his own laws. Since the state is maintained by custom and law, the essence of government traces its source back to the law-giver. All authority comes from him, as a delegation of his own supreme command. The magistrate represents the king in his absence; in his presence magisterial authority becomes null and void. The senate and the assembly are informative and advisory; they are of value to the ruler, and the wise king will weigh their words, but he will use his own judgment in action. There is no constitutional provision enforcing their will upon the king. The position of the sovereign is somewhat weakened by the fact that he cannot name his heir, for succession is determined by fundamental laws, which are restrictions he must respect. During his own lifetime, however, and within very wide limits, his will is supreme; his subjects are submitted to his guidance; there is no other earthly power which has an equal claim upon their obedience.

The application of these precepts to the situation in 1576 would mean that Henry III, a man originally brilliant in intellect, but now debauched and possibly mentally unhinged, need recognize no law which he himself had made, need accept no advice from his counsellors, need heed no plaints from the Estates, might conduct the government as he saw fit, provided that he could keep within the monetary limits set by the royal revenues from the domain, and certain other taxes which had become usual. It is only fair to Bodin to note that he assumes that the king *would* conduct the government, that his theory leaves no room for the sluggard or the totally incompetent; he postulates greater ability in governing from continued exercise of governing, and superior capacity, apparently on no foundation at all, since he acknowledge the shortcomings of sons of virtuous fathers. Magistrates should carry out orders to the letter: the Estates could petition the king, or could decline subsidies (as in fact they did), but could exercise no direct control over him. The Parlementarian claim for registration of imperial ordinances would no longer be effective. Government was to be centralised in the hands of Henry III, with the succession to his brother, Bodin's patron, the duc d'Anjou.

There are, in the two works, the following obvious contradictions: *Methodus,* Chapter VI:

Thus the superior courts which are drawn in great measure from the plebs, restrain the violence of the nobles by their just decrees, and watch over both lowly and lofty with marvellous harmony: but people who have attempted to overthrow this prestige are seeking the ruin of the state, since in these [courts] is centred the safety of domestic concord, of laws and customs, finally of the whole kingdom.[1] . . . Of all the laws of empire, none is more sacred than that one which prevents the decrees of the prince from having any force unless it is in keeping with equity and truth, for the magistrates would reject it. . . . . Often the voice of the magistrates is heard, saying "The prince can do nothing contrary to law".[2]

But in the *Republic,* Book II Chapter I, we find

This notion of a mixed state has taken such hold of men's minds that some are persuaded that this very kingdom of France, than which nothing more monarchical can be imagined, is a blend of three types: they attribute aristocracy to the Parlement of Paris, democracy to the Estates: this opinion is not only absurd, but indicates a capital error. It is a serious

[1] *Methodus*, p. 306.

[2] *Ibid.*, p. 251.

fault, to make subjects equal to the king in authority and power, or to let them share his rule. . . . A decree is not the work of magistrate or judge, but simply of the prince. . . . . The Chancellor does not announce that such and such a thing seems best to judges or to Parlement, but with a clear voice says: Rex vobis dicit.[1]

In both works he agrees that magistrates should have a long term of office, but for different reasons: in the *Methodus,* because they are thereby independent of the caprice of the prince, and can effectively check him,[2] in the *Republic,* because they are free to judge impartially—the people, not the prince.[3]

With regard to the coronation oath, he says in the *Methodus*

The consecration vow of our kings seems to me most beautiful, because the prince swears that he will give law and render justice to all. . . . Nor indeed can he violate his oath, for Right is the same for him as for a private citizen, and he is held by the same laws.[4]

Whereas in the *Republic*

The vow of our kings, which is the briefest and finest which can be made, contains nothing about the maintenance of the laws and customs of the country. . . . One can see . . . that there is no obligation to preserve the laws.[5]

[1] *De la république* (Paris, 1599), p. 265.

[2] *Methodus,* p. 159.

[3] *De la république,* Chapter IV, Book IV (Paris, 1599), p. 591.

[4] Formula ... initiationis regum nostrorum ... pulcerrima visa mihi est ... quod Princeps ... iurat se omnibus ordinibus debitam legem ac justitiam redditurum ... neque vero iuratus fidem violare facile potest ... ius enim illi dicitur ut privato cuique et iisdem legibus tenetur. *Methodus,* p. 204.

[5] Le serment de nos Roys, qui est le plus beau, et le plus bref qui se peut faire, ne port rien de garder les loix et coustumes du pays ny des predecesseurs.... On peut voir, qu'il n'y a aucune obligation de garder les loix.... De la république (Paris, 1576), p. 135.

It is possible to reconcile these on the technicality that the former refers to new laws, the latter to old, but the spirit of the one breathes recognition of control, of the other, self-sufficiency.

His opinion of the Estates also has altered: in the *Methodus* he says "[The prince] cannot uproot the laws peculiar to the whole empire, or make any change whatsoever in the customs of the state and the ancient ways, without the consent of the three estates".[1] In the *Republic:*

> As for the customs peculiar to each locality, and to the empire as a whole, which do not concern the mechanism of the kingdom, there usually had been no change without assembling the general Estates, and also those of the bailliage affected: not that it was necessary to follow their advice, or that the king could not do the contrary of that which was asked, if his native reason and justice seemed to indicate.[2]

In sum, in 1566 this was Bodin's ideal for the government of France:

> The more you take away from the power of the prince (in this direction there can be no mistake) the more just the authority and the more stable it will become. . . . Those who think they are going to increase the power of the prince by craft do not judge rightly, since they are bringing about the overthrow of king and kingdom. Indeed it is most important for the empire that the prince-ship should be kept within the power of the law.[3]

But ten years later he thinks that

> The prince moderates all things according to his will and wish; whatsoever he decrees and commands has the force of law.

[1] *Methodus*, p. 204.

[2] *De la république* (Paris, 1576), p. 138.

[3] *Methodus*, p. 261.

So very little attention ought to be given to the opinion of those men who think that the prince is checked by the power of the people. They are offering revolutionary material to seditious men, and bringing trouble to the state.[1]

Was it because of this change of view, that Bodin declared it was possible to alter an opinion honorably, to acknowledge one's self in the wrong, rather than to defend his stand stubbornly?[2] There are at least two main reasons which might account for the swerve from constitutional monarchy to an absolutism, tempered by some fundamental restrictions, but without any human agency for enforcement. One reason is private, the other public. In 1566, Bodin was a modest barrister, but recently arrived from Toulouse. He had no court connections; such friends as he had made were jurists like himself, possibly Parlementarians, jealous of their ancient traditions and anxious to extend their prerogatives. (The *Methodus* was dedicated to the president of the cour des enquêtes). In this independent situation he was free to express his real opinions, provided they were not too radical. In the midst of an historical disquisition, covering the facts and tendencies of ancient times, it was easy to convey here and there a comment on present-day affairs, or a suggestion for future improvement, without danger of being ranked as an iconoclast. Of that, there was not a trace in Bodin. He conformed to both church and state, with a reservation of criticism in a mind that could not cease to question.

But by 1576 his circumstances had altered. He had held various posts in the service of the king. He was attached to the household of the king's brother and presumptive heir. In view of these appointments, it was plainly unwise to make any attempt to curb the royal power. Indeed. it was

[1] *De Republica* (Frankfort, 1641), p. 140.

[2] See page 135 *supra*.

probably policy for a comparatively poor man like Bodin, to take up the cudgels in favor of the monarchy, particularly in view of the stream of Huguenot pamphlets which had been flooding the country since St. Bartholomew. His was not an heroic character; he would not count the world well lost for a principle, and his habitual caution would advise the repudiation of the more liberal viewpoint of his thirties. This lack of moral courage to uphold his convictions is well illustrated in a letter of 1590, where he explains his reasons for joining the League.

There was also the wider consideration of public advantage. The first civil war had ended with the death of the Duke of Guise in 1563. France was at peace while Bodin was writing the *Methodus,* so that he was free, not only in his private interests, but also in relation to concerns of state. The kingdom was hardly tranquil, but the treaty of Amboise had permitted the exercise of the Huguenot cult in one town of each baillage and in the noble manors. While non-conformists were agitating for further relief, and asking equality, rather than mere toleration, there were no actual hostilities, and it was therefore justifiable for a man with a sincere love of his country, to indicate that its government was still open to improvement. Ten years later, after two more outbreaks of internecine strife, and the massacre of 1572, the administration was hardly strong enough to withstand the criticism that it met from all sides. Before the actual publication of the *Republic,* the Politiques had risen in the south; the Catholic party was forming rudimentary groups which were later to become the League;[1] and there was a warfare of pamphlets, spreading abroad dangerous doctrines of federalism, and tyrannicide. It was time for some one to step forward in support of the government. Certainly the king and his administration had many flaws, but when

[1] R. Chauviré, *Jean Bodin* (La Flèche, 1914), p. 439.

foreigners were waiting at the borders, eagerly eyeing the anarchy within, wise men anxious to preserve the existence of the fatherland would advocate a dictator. This was practically what Bodin did. To justify extraordinary powers, he invested the ruler with a divine sanction, which was entirely consistent with the ethical aims he had expressed elsewhere. It was for this reason that he disparaged those who had written of the importance of Parlement or Estates, and accused them of a desire to overthrow the state. Exactly that they would have done if self-expression had been the order of the day, while Spain waited at the frontier. Although Bodin's dictator has sweeping powers, his semi-divine character rather precludes any vicious exercise of authority. The author constantly refers to the wisdom and justice of the sovereign, who may reject any advice offered by counsellors, if his superior enlightenment can suggest a better course. There is never a hint that this greater freedom to act may be abused. Perhaps the affirmative attitude was intended as an inspiration. Machiavelli's teachings are held up to scorn.

He boasts of being an atheist; as for knowledge, I verily believe that those who are accustomed to discuss seriously, weigh sensibly, and make sharp distinctions in matters of state, will agree that he knows not even the elements of political science, which do not lie in tyrannical strategy, that he has sought in every corner of Italy, and like a poison filtered through his book *The Prince*. There he lauds to the sky and places as a paragon above all kings the most disloyal son of a priest who ever lived; who nevertheless, with all his arts, was shamefully hurled from the slippery peak of tyranny . . . as has happened to other princes, who have followed in his footprints, and tried the fine rules of Machiavelli. He made the two bases of the state, impiety and injustice, saying that the exercise of religious principles was contrary to the success of the government.

. . . It is . . . a sad incongruity, and weighted with disaster, to teach princes the rules of injustice, to strengthen by tyranny an authority which can have no more dangerous foundation.[1]

The early reviews of the *Republic,* and particularly those from Switzerland caused the author some pain. He felt that the charge of absolutist was unfair, and that he was decidedly misunderstood. A letter written to his friend Du Faur (3 October, 1580?) congratulating him on his appointment as president of Parlement, is printed in a later, Latin edition of the Republic, and contains the following autobiographical passages:

When a year ago [sic] I wrote . . . the Republic, I thought that I had done a work pleasing to all good men, yet two kinds of reproach are levelled against me; one is from those who bicker . . . about trifling things,

the other is from those who published the second edition in Geneva.

What did I write which is contrary to the dignity . . . of that state? . . . I wonder that they think I have given somewhat more to the power of one man than befits a valiant citizen in a state, for everywhere . . . but particularly in the first book, chapter eight . . . I did not hesitate to refute those . . . who wrote about the law of fiscus and the increase of regalia in these most perilous times, because they were giving infinite power to the king, above all human and divine laws.[2]

He emphasises the three limitations which he has set upon the sovereign.

What could be more democratic than what I dared to write, that the king was not permitted to exact tribute without the consent of the citizens? Of how great importance is the fact

[1] Bodin, *De la république* (Paris, 1576), Introduction, no pagination.

[2] *De Republica* (Cologne, 1608), *Epistola,* no pagination.

which likewise I stated,—that princes are held by divine and natural law, by a sterner bond than are their subjects? That they are held by compacts just like the other citizens?

Jurisconsults frequently maintained the contrary, but Bodin justified his point of view.

When I saw everywhere subjects in arms against their princes, books equally offered, just as torches to set fire to the state,—books in which we are taught to drive from command under pretext of tyranny princes who have been sent to mankind by divine influence; likewise that kings are not descended from the royal family, but must be elected; that we should overturn . . . the restrictions, not only of this kingdom, but the foundations of all empires, I denied that it was the part of a good man, or a good citizen, to attack his prince, no matter how tyrannical. . . . Any way, my own freedom and integrity in public activity will vindicate me from this charge. The thing speaks for itself. When I was sent as delegate to the French assembly, I fought for the welfare of the people against the resources of the mighty, not without danger to my own head. I resisted the renewal of civil war, that menace to the homes of the people. I was the means of preventing the appointment of a delegate to be present at the [royal] discussion on the cahiers; this move had been agreed upon almost unanimously by all the orders, since it seemed advantageous to, but was really against, public interests. I went to the clergy and the nobles at the request of our order, and persuaded them to abandon their proposed plan.

But when they wanted to sell the domain at auction, in perpetual alienation, and to double the taxes under pretext of lessening them, I intervened, and when the king found that he could obtain nothing, he said . . . . that Bodin not only disagreed with his wishes, but had swayed his colleagues. Yet if I had been procurator of the king at the time, I could not have felt otherwise. . . .

Moreover when I could not be entrapped by any snares, all the towns of Vermandois, who in my absence had elected me against my wishes . . . . sent procurators to the assembly, to recall Bodin from his task, if possible, on the ground that he wanted to maintain two religions in the state. . . .

People who have heard that I was to be appointed maître des requêtes will understand how much my own interests have suffered. Although I preferred popular advantage to royal rewards and honors, yet I execrate those who are trying to lay hands on their leader under the plea of tyranny, to suggest the election of kings by popular suffrage, and to snatch the scepter from the hands of their lawful princes.[1]

The policy of Catherine de Medici demanded an alliance with at least one of the Protestant powers who might otherwise furnish assistance to the rebellious Calvinists. She had for some time been negotiating with England for a marriage between her youngest son and the reigning Queen. Elizabeth with her usual adroitness kept this suitor on tenterhooks for several years, during which he made two visits to London. On the second of these, in 1581, his maître des requêtes Bodin accompanied him. Subsequent editions of the *Republic* revised by the author show a pardonable vanity in his travels, since he frequently quotes his English experiences. Apparently he had made a speech to the Queen, for he says

The heavier the punishment you inflict [in religious matters], the less you will accomplish; there exists in men a deep-seated impulse and quality, making them wish to be led willingly to accept a given course; they object to being driven. This was my statement to Elizabeth the queen of the English, and to the lords and councillors when the trial was held of the Jesuit Campanius and some Catholics.[2]

The superior resources of the Parliament could not fail to impress him.

[1] *De Republica* (Cologne, 1608), *Epistola,* no pagination.

[2] *De Republica* (Frankfort, 1641), p. 755.

The queen of the English maintains her kingdom in unbelievable magnificence, and collects immense wealth in her treasury (96,000 sestercies), which is brought in yearly from the revenue of domain and ancient dues: so far from demanding tribute, as they used to do every third year, or every year, she remits it: for when I went over there with the embassy, I took great interest in attending the Parliament. Five hundred sestercies were offered by the people as tribute to be used for necessities of state, but the queen refused half the sum, and thanked her people.[1]

Did he mentally contrast Elizabeth's economy with Henry's prodigality? He returned their hospitality with kind words, for in the discussion of racial characteristics he comments that "the English were once very fierce, but due to the lasting peace they have devoted themselves to culture (I speak from experience) so that no one could be more gentle or polished." [2]

Fortune dealt him a hard blow in the premature death of his patron in 1584. Further preferment was no longer attainable. He had succeeded some time after 1577 [3] to the post of his brother-in-law, procurator of the king in the bailliage and presiding bench of Laon; he resigned his ambitions, and settled down to work in the provincial town. There is extant a letter, showing another side of Bodin. It is addressed to his nephew, and deals with the education of his children.

When I returned from England, I found them at the age of three and four respectively. Then I taught them, with nuts and cherries to name in Latin everything that they saw, and observing that they had memory and a quick wit, I commenced to teach them in Latin, the angels, the shadows, the light, the

[1] *De Republica* (Frankfort, 1641), p. 1055.

[2] *Ibid.*, p. 810.

[3] See Ponthieu, "Jean Bodin", *Revue du seizième siècle,* XV (1928) 56.

world and its age (that is, 5534 years), the sky, how many heavens there are, how many fixed and visible stars, planets and their motions.[1]

When he went away on legal business, they did not progress so well.

He had been urged to translate the *Republic* into Latin by his friend the Count of Dampierre, who said that the dignity of the matter demanded that it should be couched in the splendor of the Roman speech, both because the Romans alone had subordinated natural and fatherly love to the rights of the sovereign and the State, and also because it was only just to allies and foreigners that it be written in that language which is the common bond of literature and culture. At the time Bodin had been too much occupied with the activities of his patron, but when he found, on his visit to England, that the undergraduates at Cambridge were reading the French version " in a difficult and burdensome fashion ", he decided to undertake the work. At the death of the Duke of Anjou, when he had a little more leisure and " hardly any medecine was effective in deadening the sadness ", he set his hand to the task, using " a style simple and familiar without elaboration " since he wished to reach as large an audience as possible. In his earlier preface he had criticised those who were attacking the state. In 1584, he comments rather despondently on the state itself.

While I have been considering bygone perils and those yet to come, I began to pity our country, and to feel ashamed of an administration which, while they quarrel among themselves . . . offers so shameful a spectacle of themselves and of us to the enemies laughing at our gates.

Though adversity had driven him to take up a narrower

[1] Bibl. Nat., Fonds Latin 6564.

philosophy, there had been a day when he had visualised a world state as a means of insuring peace. Even as the king of Spain had many provinces beneath his rule, each with different laws, languages and customs, yet united in the common law of the empire, so

all kingdoms, empires, tyrannies, and states are united by the rule of reason and international law. Hence it follows that this world is like a state, and all men are in a certain sense bound together by the same sense of right, because they feel that they are kin, and all subject to one and the same Reason.

But there is little hope of immediate fulfillment, for " since that rule of reason can compel no one, it is not possible to make one State from all nations ".[1]

His philosophic dreams, and his golden means of compromise were rudely shattered at the end. In 1587, he was arrested by order of the procureur général of Parliament. La Démonomanie des Sorciers, which was published in 1580 could have laid him open to a charge of magic. We do not know the details, but he was absolved by the testimony of ten witnesses, including two priests.

Worse was in store. He had upheld religious toleration throughout his life. Sincerely devout, he defended no definite church, but outwardly conformed to that which had prescriptive rights in France. This attitude had awakened the suspicions of the more bigoted. He had been accused of sorcery; sometimes of atheism, of Calvinism. After 1588, either would have been fatal, in fact it was fatal to

[1] Omnia autem omnium regna, imperia, tyrannides, Respublicae, non alio quam rationis imperio ac gentium communi iure copulantur. Ex quo sequitur, hunc mundum veluti civitatem aliquam esse, et omnes homines eodem iure quodammodo confusos, quod intelligunt se esse consanguineos, et subiectos omnes sub unam eandemque rationis tutelam. Sed quia illud imperium rationis cogit neminem revera non potest una ex omnibus gentibus Respublica conflari. *Methodus*, p. 166.

be tolerant in the town of Laon. The power of the king was waning; the power of the League was waxing. From Paris came the order to join the revolt against the vacillating rule of Henry III, to follow instead the positive program of the League. It had been formed originally to put down the Huguenots; after 1584 it was revived to prevent the succession of a Huguenot king. Their manifesto, published in 1585, proclaimed not only the danger to the faith, but also the corruption and inefficiency of the government, and was aimed equally at Henry of Valois and Henry of Navarre. It demanded a session of the Estates General every three years.[1]

The royal governor was too weak to withstand the forces of ultramontanism; he yielded, and the king's procurator likewise. Bodin actually delivered an address by which he sought to overcome the hesitancy of his fellow citizens. He refused to obey orders sent him by the king, recognising only the authority of Cardinal de Lorraine as lieutenant general of the crown of France. It is not easy to believe that this was a sincere change of opinion. The whole tenor of his life had been conservative, royalist, not persecuting; but the followers of the League in Laon were drawn from the poorer class, that rabble whom he so much despised. They made no pretense of their suspicions of the wealthy or the pacific; a fair amount of class consciousness was mingled with superstitious fervor, and Bodin feared for life and home. There was a statement issued by him in 1590, purporting to defend his acceptance of the League, but one cannot fail to note a certain tepidity in his enthusiasm.

Being in a town, it is obligatory to belong to the strongest party . . . or one is completely ruined. To be sure I sup-

[1] F. Rocquain, *La France et Rome pendant les guerres de religion* (Paris, 1924), p. 273.

ported the party of the late king as long as my duty and honor permitted, until I saw that I was on the verge of being killed, with two hundred others who defended the king, if I did not obey the arrêt of Parlement, which had been sent me for the second time by the procureur general; in addition, two men had made an attempt to shoot me. . . .

As for the justice of the cause: who can doubt that the Catholics have been in possession for 1600 years. Is that not enough to establish prescriptive rights? . . . As for the state . . . . the royal law gives the crown to the nearest house in a direct line from the royal. This is in conformity with divine law. Now the Cardinal de Bourbon descends from St. Louis, by his son Robert of Clermont, in the thirteenth degree, but the king of Navarre in the fourteenth degree. Of course they say that the king of Navarre succeeds by representation [of his father], but that is a new-fangled jurisprudence. . . . I assert that the crown of France is not hereditary . . . this is a law of empire, which could have been denied, but having once been accepted, cannot be abandoned or altered.[1]

In very recent times there has been discovered a document indicating that Bodin had not always been so neglectful of the interests of the King of Navarre. In the Picardy register [2] is a letter from the Chambre des Comptes de La Fère, dated November 2nd, 1587, and making him avocat and councillor in the bailliage of Laon for the affairs of the county of Marle, which belonged to Navarre. Reference is repeatedly made to the many services which Bodin had rendered to both the King and Queen of Navarre. The recipient has written in the margin, characteristically enough, " Pour estre du Conseil du Roy de Navarre. Il y a pension. Me est deub ung an et demy. Fait le Ve avril V^cIIII^xxIX ".

By walking warily, and prevaricating on occasion, he succeeded in carrying on. In the latter months of 1594, Henry

[1] Bibl. Nat., Fonds Francais 20153.

[2] See footnote page 105, *supra*.

of Navarre and his allies the Politiques were guiding the destinies of France. With them Bodin was in fullest sympathy; they represented exactly that path of compromise under benevolent despotism which he had supported,—except indeed during those last few years of danger. Laon became once more a quiet retreat. His literary labors were quickened; the *Theatrum Naturae,* composed "Gallia tota bello civili flagrante", was published in the Spring of 1596, and some works in manuscript, notably the *Heptaplomeres,* were discovered after his death in June. From vanity or caution, he had burned earlier works on jurisprudence and sovereignty. Although the unpublished *Heptaplomeres,* which would certainly have brought rapid ruin if discovered by the Leaguers, had portrayed an astonishing impartiality to creeds of all sorts, even Mohammedan and Jewish, nevertheless he requested burial in the chapel of the Cordeliers as a final tribute to conformity and to tradition.

CONCLUSION

ANY comparison of the characters of these two authors must note at once the striking dissimilarity of temperament, which is the basis of their differences in political philosophy. The Teutonic blood of Hotman must at some time have been mingled with that of the Celt, for emotion, whether spiritual or mundane, was a primary ingredient in the motivation of his activities. As an impressionable youth he had come in contact with Calvin, who had inflamed his ardent soul with the abuses of Romanism, and the purity of the ancient faith. Impulsive and restless though he was in the frequent decisions of his career, to this one lofty ideal he fearlessly directed his steps, and his constancy in this regard is the more noble in that it cost him so dearly. In matters of this world, he exemplified that individualism so typical of the sixteenth century; he was impatient of control; he could not accept the abstract rectitude of an order *de par le roi* that controlled the destinies of 16,000,000 other human beings. This independence, this claim for self-expression which is pre-eminently of the modern world, drove him logically to the thesis that the right to rule rests with the Three Estates, that only by the integration of these separate authorities do we achieve a single authority that is both lawful and unique. Even then it must be guided by constant contact with the creating power, and when out of touch and sympathy should be renewed. The eighteenth century elaborated this by extending the possession of authority to the masses, but added nothing new. Furthermore the mind of Hotman was incomparably clearer and more logical than the mind of Rousseau.

Forming an effective contrast stood Bodin, cool-headed, sagacious, reluctant to gamble or to burn his boats behind him, devout in his acceptance of a directing Principle throughout the universe, which he did not care to define precisely in any creed, more amenable to guidance, hence, in his acceptance of authority, more medieval. He had a deeper mind that Hotman, something more than mere brain; if one glances at the list of his works, it is apparent that he had a concept of the one-ness of the Universe, that he deals separately with all the important fields of knowledge, history, law, politics, sorcery, science, in order at last to blend them and to superimpose upon this earthly framework an all-pervading Providence which knows no distinction of church or creed. Hotman could not extend himself so far; as he was more modern, so was he more superficial.

It is therefore quite consistent with his temperament that Bodin should portray the king of France as all powerful within his earthly sphere. Continuity would force him to take this stand. If he was conscious that the universe was indissolubly linked, then the relations which exist between God and his creatures, must exist also between that being whom God permits to rule on earth, e.g., in France, and his creatures. Due to the exigencies of the situation, this earthly guidance is only semi-divine, and in recognition of possible flaws in the human agent, Bodin recommends, indeed recommends rather highly, the assistance of intellectuals in an advisory capacity, and, to insure eager obedience, the assistance of the Estates in an informatory capacity, since men have a disconcerting habit of preferring to be led rather than driven. Hotman would have made both these function compulsory and binding.

They fundamentally disagree in their conception of sovereignty. Hotman evades discussion of this idea, but it is after all inevitable and implicit in any treatment of the State.

Bodin gives it many titles, but does not so clearly tell what he thinks it is, as what he thinks it does. Perhaps to him it means the manifestation of Providential rule in the state, therefore all-wise, unquestionable. Its attributes are functions involving a delegation of power for executive purposes, but no final authority, which remains at the source. From this flows his (Austinian) definition of (statute) law as the enunciation of the will of the sovereign. By extending the application of this idea, we may infer the relation of the king to God, and hence the upper limits of his authority. No earthly power really is sovereign, but as the head of the state is the nearest approach on earth to the Deity, he has supreme command over his subjects, and right to demand unhesitating obedience.

Hotman had not so coherent a philosophy. He was passionately religious; he wished the state to further God's will on earth, but he felt that the channel of communication was not through one individual man, but through many. This would entail, so far as France was concerned, a threefold division of authority for the promulgation of law: initiation by the Estates, expression by the king, confirmation by Parlement. None was supreme in itself. No policy could legally be formulated without the exercise of the three complementary functions. The refusal of any one body blocked both the others.

The origin of government for Bodin was quite logically force, or a unilateral compact. Equally consistent with *his* aims, was Hotman's explanation of a bilateral contract, revocable upon violation by either party to the contract.

Their respective understanding of the incidence of sovereignty determined of course their ideas of the nature of kingship. Bodin took over from the middle ages his concept of the semi-divinity of royalty, his theory of power flowing from the summit down. In his implicit assumption that the king will choose the best way, either from his own creative wisdom, or by selection from the proffered wisdom of his councillors, there is an inheritance from ancient times. Hotman in supporting a more democratic principle, was reverting to the days of primitive Christianity, and advocating a theory that only a very few of the bolder minds of the Middle Age had dared to conceive. The king was the material instrument of the power of the people. Authority came to him from below, as a rising vapor.

What was to be done if the executive head was not maintaining the divine law on earth? Bodin's conception of kingship of course makes removal impossible. The tyrant has been sent by God, who sends the just ruler also; we must suffer in acknowledgment of God's will. The individual is but a pigmy in the might of the universe. Bodin's only concession would be in the case of an official who had merely precarious tenure. Here there is a clear reservation of authority; the official is not sovereign, and may be removed or even killed. The machinery which Hotman had set up for control of the government would hardly permit the legal existence of tyranny, but if the king, by show of force, were to gain complete control, and issue ordinances without the proper sanctions, he could be deposed by the Estates General.

They differed greatly in their attitude toward their mother country. Perhaps it is not fair to contrast them on this point, for conditions were not the same, and Hotman could hardly consider that he owed much fealty to the land that had exiled him for using his own mind in spiritual matters. Nevertheless, in Lausanne and in Geneva, we find him constantly reverting to the situation in France, calling her " Gallia nostra ". In 1563 he seized the first opportunity to return, as a matter of course, to pick up his life where he had left it in 1547. But the massacre drove him forth forever. He had no compunction in watching the penetration of the

English, in fact he tried to assist La Rochelle in what was practically treason; he was in communication with the German princes, constantly urging them to interfere in French domestic affairs. The Spanish encroachments of course he condemned as they were supporting the Catholic party. But in this never ending solicitation of men and money, he seems to have been sublimely unconscious of the fact that he was working against France; that foreigners would take their reward in annexation of territory; that the incessant warfare might end not only in the disappearance of the French government, which, as it then was, he detested, but also in the disappearance of France itself. Would he have cared? Would he have sacrificed his religious interests to his national pride? Apparently his patriotism had not reached that pitch of white-hot fervor.

As for Bodin, it is indeed difficult to picture him in a moment of exuberance, excitedly waving a flag. And yet, metaphorically speaking, that is what he did. He had had in 1566 a plan of definite limitations for the monarchy; it was a highly centralized government, to be sure, but with constitutional safeguards. By 1576, he had rejected this for a much less qualified absolutism. Why? In his own words, because of the sale of seditious books "like torches to set fire to the state". At Blois, he had opposed the alienation of state land, in the face of royal disfavor. A few years later, having watched Henry III waver from one faction to another, until there was no cohesion, no force, no guidance left in the government, he commented sadly on "the foreigners laughing idly at our gates" and eventually threw in his lot with the group which seemed to control the majority.

Despite this disagreement, Hotman and Bodin had some common bonds of interest. Both were scholars, with a similar mental furnishing. To quote Monod, "Francois Hotman and Jean Bodin, who dedicated a vast historical erudition to the service of their political passions, were, the one a Calvinist, the other . . . a rare mind of a singular boldness."[1] They employed their independence of thought in different ways, but their knowledge of history gave them a common predilection for the past, and a common desire to see it projected into the present. In their interpretation of the past they admittedly differ. Bodin saw in the kingship of the early days, a paternal despotism, a judge sagely directing his people, and hoped to perpetuate this. Hotman saw, or perhaps wanted to see, because it better served his needs, an elective monarchy, restrained by the votes of the comitia. This had once been the order for France; therefore it should exist again.

There was common agreement on ethical principles. The government should devote itself to the improvement of its subjects to crushing oppression and maintaining justice. It was the nearest possible approach to the rule of Divine law on earth. They joined heartily in abhorrence of the precepts of Machiavelli. They concurred also in the moral aims of the individual citizen, in the value of his sense of responsibility, although they differed in the amount of co-operation they would allow. For the lowest class they had a uniform contempt.

Finally they agreed in the ruler's capacity of trustee, although in the one case he held in trust for God, in the other for the people. This is exemplified chiefly in the insistence upon recognition of fundamental law, and upon the financial position of the king. The land from which he draws his sustenance belongs to the nation; the aides and other taxes which constitute the fisc are to be used for the upkeep of the government; he may have nothing in addition without the consent of the Estates. (Bodin upheld this not only in

[1] G. Monod, "Du progrès des sciences historiques", *La Revue Historique*, I (1876), 5.

theory, but in practice.) Whether he be divinely ordained or not, a rigid compliance with these conditions would shackle his activities considerably.

In conclusion, one must necessarily comment on the strength and longevity of the constitutional movement in France. Like a certain famous personage, it took "an unconscionably long time" in dying. In the fourteenth century, it had made demands quite as sweeping as those of the parallel movement across the Channel. In the fifteenth, there had been spasmodic revivals; in the sixteenth, under the combined influence of religious, economic, and political discontent (a combination which did not seriously affect England until the following century) there was a steady current of resistance to monarchial supremacy which only just missed attaining its goal.

What restrictions actually were in practice? In default of any written constitutional law, this cardinal point cannot be established. We have in many cases, a procès verbal, or a journal describing the proceedings of the Estates. We can learn what they actually did do, but this source of information does not indicate whether or not compulsion was brought upon them to desist, whether they maintained their rights, or overstepped them. Judging from the statement of Philip de Commines, and from the conduct of the Estates of 1576, it was an accepted law that no unusual tribute could be levied without the approval of that assembly. Two other laws which must have been recognised, since they were upheld in the face of difficulties, were (1) the succession to the throne of the eldest male descended from the eldest male and (2) non-alienation of public land without public consent. One restriction that lay on the border line between law and vanishing custom was the Parlementary registration of royal edicts. This must still have been recognised, at least as a necessary formality, for both the Edict of Toleration of

1562 and the Peace of Monsieur of 1576, being refused by Parlement, were forced through by a *lit de justice*.

There were some other limitations upon the power of the king which had perhaps been effective in the past, but were so no longer; among these might be named, the special authority given to the Estates in the king's minority, the periodical assembly of the Estates General, the right of the provincial Estates to regulate the amount of taxation within their own boundaries, and the co-option by the maîtres in Parliament of three nominees for vacancies in office. Some sessions of the Estates had upheld the theory that no two houses could combine to force through a measure which the third rejected. This could not be adequately enforced, but the arrangements for the Estates of Languedoc conducted under the supervision of the Politiques were undoubtedly intended to correct this injustice to the Tiers.

It is surprising to note the unanimity of the various factions on the type of constitutional safeguards which should be imposed. Bitter as was their animosity for religious reasons, they could not fail to observe how little their own interests were served by an inefficient, rudderless, and yet independent monarch. There was no driving force in the government and no cooperation to insure a resultant. The Estates of Pontoise had asked a convocation every two years. In 1566, the *Methodus* had called attention to the need for stabilisation; in 1573, *Franco-Gallia,* written by a member of the opposing faction had suggested the Estates General as a means to that end. The Politiques of the South, fighting from 1574 to 1576, had asked the regular summoning of the Estates as one of the conditions of peace. The Estates of Blois, that met as a consequence of this treaty, represented the moderate Catholic party, but they also asked that the assembly be made part of the constitutional machinery through the regulation that any unanimous request should automatically become law. Although Bodin in this same year modified his State in the direction of greater centralisation, he denied that he had any intention of making monarchical authority limitless. The platform of the League of 1585 stated that in the common interest, the Estates General should meet at least once every three years. Finally, Henry III, in his address to the second Estates of Blois (1588) said in part "If it seems that . . . I submit too easily to the laws of which I am the author, although it is acknowledged that I am free from their control, and that by this means I render the royal dignity in any way less supreme than that of my predecessors; it is in this very thing that the true generosity of a good prince reveals itself,— to moderate his thoughts and actions in accordance with equity. . . . I am content to answer, with that king whom they blamed for leaving less power to his successors than he had received from his ancestors—that he was by that very means leaving the power more assured and lasting." [1]

It is unfortunate, in view of this surprising concord in the field of practical politics, that no effective steps were taken to create a constitutional monarchy with at least aristocratic checks, but that instead, France sank under an absolute control which was shattered only by revolution.

[1] *Actes de la seconde séance des Estats Gênéraux tenus à Blois* (Paris, 1588), p. 9.

BIBLIOGRAPHY OF WORKS UTILISED

Sources

Actes de la seconde séance des Estats Généraux tenus à Blois (Paris, 1588).

Pierre de Rémi, sieur de Beaumanoir, *Coustumes de Beauvaisis*, Edition Beugnot (Paris, 1842).

Théodore de Bèze, *Histoire ecclésiastique des Églises réformées* (Antwerp, 1580).

Jean Bodin:

Letters in MS.
- Brit. Mus. Egerton Collection 17 Plut. 525 K. Bodin to Bignon.
- Bibl. Nat. Fonds Latin 6564. Bodin on the education of his children.
- Bibl. Nat. Fonds Français 20153. Bodin's reasons for joining the League.

in print
- *La Revue du seizième siècle*, XV (1928) 56-90.

Works
- *Methodus ad facilem historiarum cognitionem* (Lyons, 1583).
- *De la République* (Paris, 1576).
- —— (Paris, 1599). For the Apologie de René Herpin.
- —— (Cologne, 1608). For the Epistola Vido Fabro.
- *De Republica* (Frankfort, 1641).
- *Recueil de tout ce qui s'est negotié en la compagnie du Tiers Estat de France tenus à Blois*, 1576. (s. l., 1577).
- *Response . . . au paradoxe de Malestroict, touchant l'enchérissement de toutes choses et le moyen d'y remédier* (Paris, 1578).

Jean Calvin: *Corpus Reformatorum; Joannis Calvini opera quae supersunt omnia ediderunt Baum . . . Cunitz . . . Reuss* (Brunswick, 1877).

——, *Institution de la Religion Chrestienne* (Paris, 1911). From the original French edition.

Philippe de Commines, *Mémoires*, Edition Mandrot (Paris, 1901).

De la necessité d'assembler les Estats (Paris, 1567).

Charles Du Moulin, *Coustumes de la Prévosté et Vicomté de Paris* (Paris, 1691).

Du Haillan, seigneur, *Conditions sous lesquelles les Français se sont donnés un Roi* (Paris, 1789).

S. Goulart, *Les Mémoires de la Ligue* (Geneva ?, 1598), vol. i.

——, *Les Mémoires de l'Estat de France sous Charles IX* (Meidelboug [sic], 1578).

François Hotman:

Letters in MS.

Basel, Oeffentliche Bibliothek, Amerbach's correspondence,
G II, 19
Fr. Gr. Ms. II, 2
Fr. Gr. Ms. II, 27
G II, 27
G II, 6
G II, 12
Fr. Gr. Ms. II, 5a
G I, 66
Fr. Gr. Ms. I, 12.

Paris, Bibliothèque Nationale, Fonds Latin 8586 and 10327. Collection Dupuy No. 729 and No. 797.

London, British Museum, Harleian Collection 4935 Vol. 68 E.

Letters in print

P. J. Blok, "Correspondance inédite de ... François Hotman", *Archives du Musée Teyler*, Série ii, vol. xii, Deuxième Partie (Haarlem, 1911).

R. Dareste, *Revue Historique de droit français et étranger*, I (1855) 492.

L. Ehinger, "Franz Hotman", *Historische Gesellschaft für Vaterländische Geschichte, Beiträge*, Neue Folge, Band iv, Heft i (vol. xiv of the complete series), (Basel, 1892).

J. C. Fuessli, *Epistolae ad* [*sic*] *Ecclesiae Helveticae Reformatoribus vel ad eos scriptae* (Zurich, 1742).

H. Hauser, *Revue Historique*, XLIII (1891) 54.

B. F. Hummel, *Celebrium Virorum Epistolae ineditae* (Nuremberg, 1777).

J. W. Meelius, *F. et J. Hotomannorum ... Epistolae* (Amsterdam, 1700).

Works

Observationum Liber primus (Basel, 1560-1561).

Epistre envoiée au Tigre de la France (s. l. n. d. 1560?). Reproduction by Ch. Read (Paris, 1875).

Opuscules (containing *Antitribonian*, fait par l'advis de feu M. de l'Hôpital, Chancelier de France, dès l'an 1567), (Paris, 1616-1593 *sic*).

De furoribus Gallicis, horrenda et indigna amirallii Castillionei nobilium atque illustrium caede (London, 1574). Translation by Timme.

La Gaule Française (Cologne, 1574).

Franco-Gallia (Frankfort, 1586).
—— (London, 1738). English translation by R. Molesworth.
Gasparis Colinii Castellonei, Magni Quondam Franciae Amirallii, Vita (s. l., 1575).
Strigilis Papirii Massoni (s. l., 1575).
Monitoriale adversus Italo-Galliam (s. l., 1578).
Protestation et Defense pour le Roy de Navarre Henry III, premier prince de France, et Henry Prince de Condé... contre l'injuste et tyrannique Bulle de Sixte V publiée à Romme, au mois de Septembre 1585 au mespris de la maison de France (s. l., 1587).
Ad tractatum Matthaei Zampini I. C.... De successione praerogativae primi Principis Franciae . . . Responsio (s. l., 1588).
Omnia Opera, 3 vols. (Lyons, 1599-1600).

I. L. P., *Discours sur les Estats de France, et si serait plus expedient que les Estats de France fussent annuels...* (Antwerp, 1589).
P. A. Isambert [et alii], *Recueil Général des Anciennes Lois Françaises* (Paris, 1822). Later volumes of the same work are known as *Les Ordonnances des rois de France.*
John Terrarubeus, *Tractatus de Jure Legitimi successoris in hereditate regni Galliae* (Frankfort, 1585).
Jean Juvénal des Ursins, *Chronique* (In Michaud et Poujoulat, première série, tome 2, Paris, 1836—).
M. de l'Hôpital, *Oeuvres* (Paris, 1824).
Jehan Masselin, *Journal des États Généraux de Tours*, Edition Bernier (Paris, 1835).
C. Palma-Cayet, *Chronologie Novênaire* (Paris, 1836).
Etienne Pasquier, *Lettres* (Paris, 1619).
Picot and Stein, *Recueil de pièces historiques imprimées sous... Louis XI.*
Recueil de pièces originales et authentiques concernant la tenue des États Généraux (Paris, 1789). 9 vols. Editors Lalourcé et Duval.
Remonstrance aux Estatz de France pour la Paix (Lyons, 1577).
G. de Saulx-Tavannes, "Corréspondance", *Mémoires de l'Académie de Dijon* (Dijon, 1877).
Claude de Seyssel, *La Grant Monarchie de France* (Paris, 1541).
A. Thierry, *Recueil des monuments inédits de l'histoire du Tiers État* (Paris, 1850).

Secondary Works

G. Abord, *La Réforme et la Ligue à Autun* (Autun, 1855-1857).
S. Armstrong, "Political Theories of the Huguenots", *English Historical Review*, IV (1889) 13.

C. T. Atkinson, *Michel de l'Hôpital* (New York, 1900).
F. Aubert, *Histoire du Parlement de Paris* (Paris, 1894).
A. Babeau, "La Représentation du Tiers État... au xvie siècle", *Revue Historique*, XXI (1883) 91.
H. M. Baird, "Hotman and Franco-Gallia", *American Historical Review*, I (1896) 696.
J. Baron, *Franz Hotman's Antitribonian:* ein Beitrag zu dem Codifications-Bestrebungen von xvi ten bis zum xvii ten Jahrhundert (Berne, 1888).
M. H. Baudrillart, *Jean Bodin:* Tableau des idées politiques et des idées économiques au seizième siècle (Paris, 1853).
René Belleval, *Les fils d'Henri* II (Paris, 1898).
——, *François* II (Paris, 1898).
E. Blocaille, *Étude sur François Hotman* (Dijon, 1902).
J. J. Boissardus, *Icones virorum illustrium... cum eorum vitis descriptis* (Frankfort, 1597-1599).
C. Charleville, *Les États Généraux de 1576* (Paris, 1901).
R. Chauviré, *Jean Bodin* (La Fléche, 1914).
——, *Colloquium Heptaplomeres de Bodin* (Traduction française), (Paris, 1914).
R. Dareste, "François Hotman", *Revue Historique,* II (1871) 1, and 367.
——, "Hotman et la Conjuration d'Amboise", *Bibliothèque de l'École des Chartes,* XV (1854) 361.
——, *Essai sur François Hotman* (Paris, 1850).
R. Doucet, *Étude sur le gouvernement de François I* (Paris, 1921).
W. A. Dunning, "Jean Bodin and Sovereignty", *Political Science Quarterly*, XI (1896), 55.
L. Ehinger, "Franz Hotman, ein französischer Gelehrter, Staatsmann und Publicist des xvi ten Jahrhunderts", *Historische Gesellschaft für Vaterländische Geschichte, Beiträge*, Neue Folge, Band iv, Heft i (Basel, 1892).
Adhémar Esmein, *Cours élémentaire d'histoire du droit français* (Paris, 1895).
H. D. Foster, *Collected Papers* (New York, 1927).
C. H. Graf, *Essai sur la vie et les écrits de J. Lefèvre d'Étaples* (Strassburg, 1885).
F. P. G. Guizot, *Les Vies de quatre grands Chrétiens français* (Paris, 1873).
J. Garnier, *Chartes des communes et d' affranchissements en Bourgogne* (Dijon, 1918).
Otto Gierke, *Political Theories of the Middle Age*, Trans. F. W. Maitland (Cambridge, 1922).
J. Guhrauer, *Das Heptaplomeres* (Berlin, 1841).
E. Haag, *La France Protestante* (Paris, 1846-1859).

Henri Hauser, "The French Reformation", *American Historical Review,* IV (1899), 217.

——, *Le traité de Madrid et la cession de la Bourgogne à Charles Quint* (Paris, 1912).

H. Hervieu, *Recherches sur les premiers États Généraux ... pendant la première moitié du quatorzième siècle* (Paris, 1879).

C. G. Kelly, *French Protestantism 1559-1562* (Baltimore, 1918).

Charles Labitte, *La Démocratie chez les prédicateurs de la Ligue* (Paris, 1841).

T. McCrie, *Life of Andrew Melville* (Edinburgh, 1819).

C. V. Langlois, *La Régne de Philippe III* (Paris, 1887).

——, "Les Origines du Parlement de Paris", *La Revue Historique,* XVII (1890) 74.

——, "English and French Institutions in the Middle Age", *English Historical Review,* V (1890), 261.

F. Maton, *La Souveraineté dans Jean Juvénal des Ursins* (Paris, 1917).

G. Monod, "Du progrès des Sciences Historiques", *Revue Historique,* I (1876), 5.

F. C. Palm, *Politics and Religion in Sixteenth Century France* (Boston, 1926).

G. Picot, *Histoire des Etats Généraux* (Paris, 1888).

F. Renz, *Jean Bodin:* ein Beitrag zur Geschichte der historischen Methode im xvi ten Jahrhundert (Gotha, 1905).

Aug. Renaudet, "Préréforme et humanisme à Paris 1494-1517", *Bibliothèque de l'Institut Francais de Florence,* Série I, tome vi, 1916.

F. Rocquain, *La France et Rome pendant les guerres de religion* (Paris, 1924).

L. Romier, *Le Royaume de Catherine de Médicis* (Paris, 1922).

——, *La Conjuration d'Amboise* (Paris, 1923).

——, *Catholiques et Huguenots à la cour de Charles IX* (Paris, 1924).

H. Hagenbuch, "Lucien Romier", *Neue Schweizer Rundschau,* October, 1926, pp. 973-977.

A. de Ruble, *Antoine de Bourbon et Jeanne d'Albret* (Paris, 1881-1886).

A. E. Shaw, *Michel de l'Hospital* (London, 1905).

D. B. Smith, "Francis Hotman", *Scottish Historical Review,* XIII (1916), 300.

T. F. Tout, Review of *Philippe III* by C. V. Langlois, *English Historical Review,* IV (1889), 365.

Noel Valois, "Le Conseil pendant la première année de Charles VIII", *Bibliothèque de l'Ecole des Chartes,* XLIII (1882), 594.

——, "Le Gouvernement représentatif en France au xive siècle", *Revue des Questions Historiques,* XXXVI (1885), 63.

P. Van Dyke, "The Estates of Pontoise", *English Historical Review,* XXVIII (1914), 493.

Paul Viollet, *Histoire des institutions politiques et administratives de la France* (Paris, 1890-1912).

H. Vuilleumier, "Le Séjour de Hotman à Lausanne 1549-1555", *Bulletin du Bibliophile,* 1901.

G. Weill, *Les Théories sur le pouvoir royal en France pendant les guerres de religion* (Paris, 1901).

INDEX